MODER
VINTAGE GIFTS

MODERN VINTAGE GIFTS

xxxxxxxxxxxxxxxxxxxxxxx

OVER 20 PRETTY & NOSTALGIC PROJECTS TO SEW & GIVE

Helen Philipps

D&C
David and Charles

www.stitchcraftcreate.co.uk

CONTENTS

DEDICATION

TO DEAR LITTLE RHYS,
WITH ALL MY LOVE

INTRODUCTION

Modern Vintage Gifts is a varied collection of handmade fabric projects inspired by traditional patchwork and sewing crafts but brought up to date with contemporary fabrics and fresh ideas.

I love to play with fabrics and colours and the effect of one fabric with another is what first appealed to me about patchwork. I learnt to do patchwork when I was still a schoolgirl and the first shapes I sewed were hexagons, which I still enjoy using. I love the old, traditional patchwork blocks and templates and finding new and modern ways to use them. Here I have stitched diamonds together to make stars, combined hexagons with appliqué and fabric flowers, sewn Big Dipper blocks for a small quilt and stitched bold tumbler shapes for stylish red and white festive pillows.

There are plenty of small projects for quick makes too (perfect for when you are short of time but still want to make a special gift), including floral and striped appliqué hearts, a bright and colourful garland of birds, fluttering butterfly gift tags, easy-sew holly coasters and a sweet, scrappy star pincushion.

I have always been fascinated by vintage fabric toys, the kind you see in museums and the nurseries of historic houses open to the public or, if you are lucky, passed down through the family. Little fabric dolls, bears and rabbits tucked into antique toy beds and prams have always charmed me, so for this book I have made a small bear, a mouse and two dolls, as well as some tiny patchwork doll quilts.

Flowers and fruits are always a crafty favourite of mine, and they appear in this book as a summery strawberry wreath, a strawberry pincushion set, a pair of autumn pillows embellished with a bright appliqué pumpkin, a red and white spotted toadstool, a big flower appliqué pillow, a set of stuffed fabric pumpkins and a fresh and pretty cherry pot holder to brighten up the kitchen.

I hope this book will inspire you to make your own projects, using the instructions and templates to make them just as they appear here, or taking the ideas and using them as a starting point for your own creativity. If you are new to sewing and crafting just jump in and have a go at any project that appeals to you. It doesn't have to be perfect and by following the simple instructions here you can soon learn how to make things and add your own special touches, too.

Happy making!

Helen

x

STRAWBERRY WREATH

Making and decorating a fabric wreath is a great way to use up scraps and left-over binding from patchwork projects. This wreath is a really lovely summer decoration with its sweet strawberries, flowers and leaves, and it's easy to make, too. You can add as many strawberries and flowers as you wish, and they are so pretty you may even want to make a few spare ones to add to other projects.

You will need

- Polystyrene ring wreath form 8in (20cm) diameter
- Striped cotton fabric 5in (12.5cm) wide x 4yd (3.75m)
- Red spotted fabric for strawberries about 6in x 8in (15cm x 20cm)
- White fabric scraps for flowers about 8in x 12in (20cm x 30.5cm)
- Scraps of white felt
- Scraps of light green and mid-green felt for leaves
- Thin card for templates
- Three small yellow buttons
- Sewing threads to suit fabrics
- Glue gun or strong fabric glue
- Polyester toy filling

FINISHED SIZE

8in (20cm) diameter approx. Use ¼in (5mm) seams unless otherwise stated

COVERING THE WREATH

1. Fold the long strip of striped cotton fabric in half, wrong sides together, and press. Roll it up into a ball. Pin the end of the fabric roll to the wrong side of the wreath with straight pins (Fig 1). Now wind the fabric round and round the wreath until it is covered evenly (Fig 2). Secure the end by pushing pins into the wreath at the back.

tip

To create your own unique wreath you could use any fabric for binding the wreath. You can make the flowers any colour you wish, too. If it's a gift for a friend, use their favourite colours.

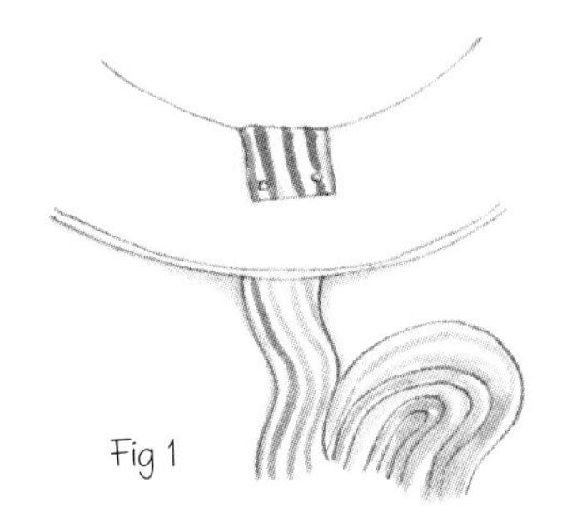

Fig 1

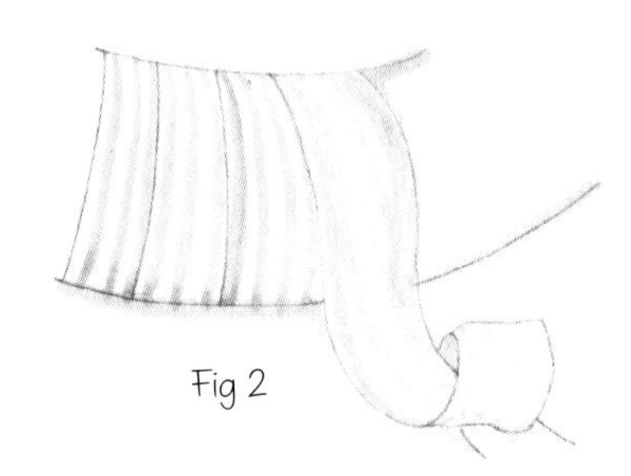

Fig 2

MAKING THE FLOWERS

2. To make a flower, cut five 2in (5cm) squares from white fabric. Fold each square in half (wrong sides together if using a white print fabric), and press with an iron (Fig 3). Take one triangle and, using white sewing thread, gather the bottom of the triangle to form a petal and secure with small stitches (Fig 4).

3. Make four more petals in the same way. Join the petals together into a circle (Fig 5). Glue a small circle of white felt onto the back of the flower, and then attach a yellow button to the centre of the flower, either by sewing or gluing it in place. Make two more flowers in the same way.

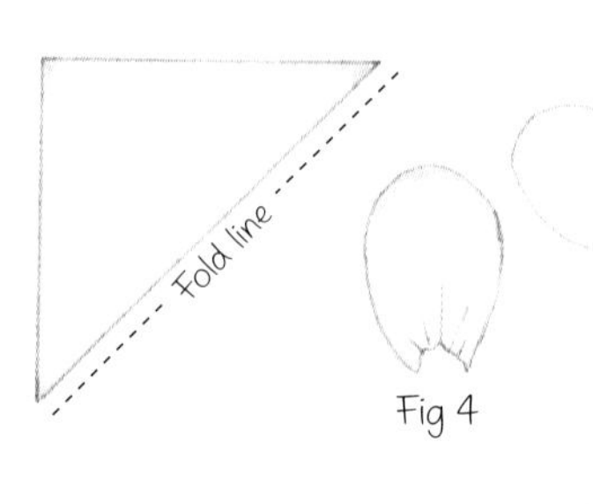

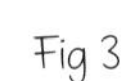

Fig 3

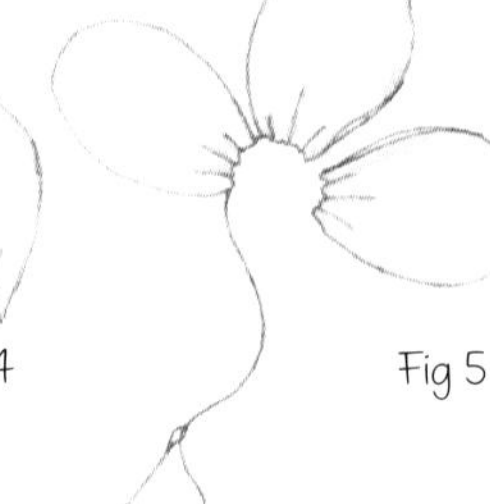

Fig 4

Fig 5

MAKING THE STRAWBERRIES

4. Use the templates to trace the shapes for the strawberries, strawberry tops and leaves onto thin card and cut out carefully.

5. To make a strawberry, draw round the strawberry template on a piece of red spotty fabric and cut out the shape (Fig 6). Fold the piece in half, right sides together, and sew the straight seam either by hand or machine (Fig 7). Turn right side out, gather the top of the strawberry with a needle and sewing thread and stuff with polyester toy filling (Fig 8). Pull the top of the strawberry tight and fasten off.

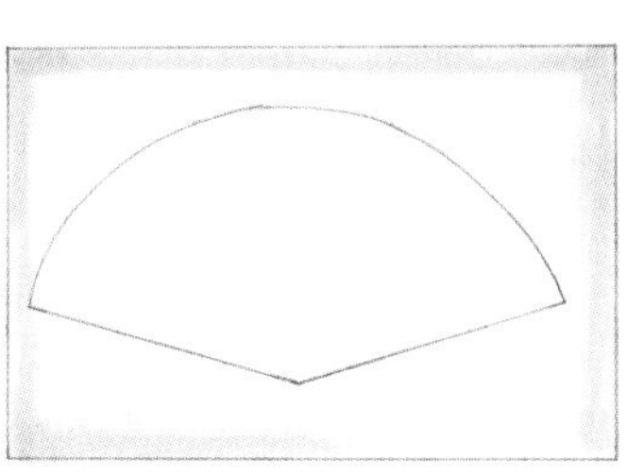

Fig 6

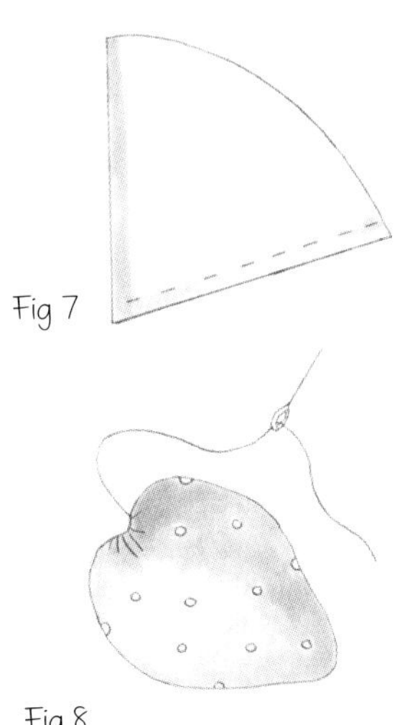

Fig 7

Fig 8

6. Use the template to cut out the strawberry top from light green felt (Fig 9). Glue or sew in place. Make two more strawberries in the same way.

Fig 9

7. Using the leaf template, draw round it onto green felt and cut out five leaves from mid-green felt and four leaves from light green felt. Arrange the leaves, flowers and strawberries as shown in the main photograph, and use a glue gun or strong fabric glue to secure each decorative element in place. To finish, use straight pins to secure a piece of ribbon to the back of the wreath for hanging.

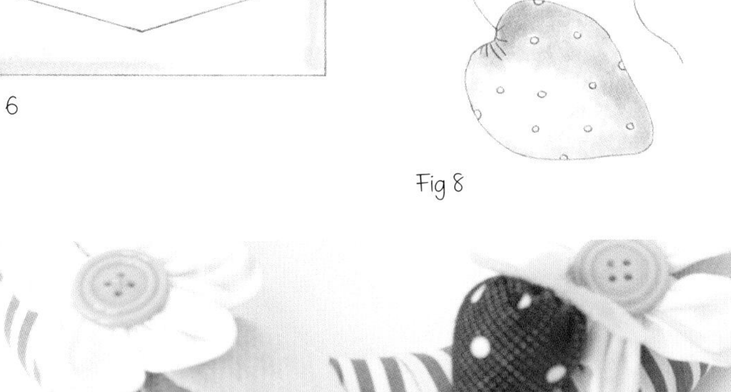

Templates (full size)

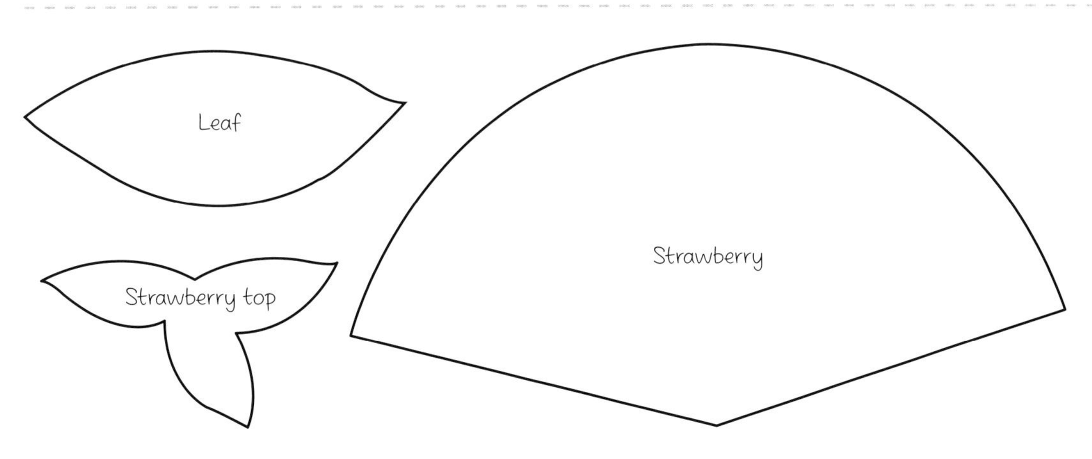

STRAWBERRY PINCUSHION & SCISSOR KEEP

This pretty little pincushion is based on a traditional Shoofly quilt block. The fresh colours and sweet strawberries in this design will make you think of summer all year round. The patchwork pincushion is simple to make and the contrasting quilting here and there gives it a pretty finish. The cute little scissor keep makes a useful additional gift to complete the set. You can play around with other strawberry prints and fabrics and create your own summer sewing set. The instructions for this project are for English paper piecing, but it could easily be sewn together by machine if you prefer.

For pincushion

- Thin card for template and scrap paper
- Scraps of blue and red floral fabrics
- Scraps of white and green fabrics
- Scraps of pink/white striped fabric
- Scraps of red spotty fabric
- Fusible web
- Lightweight wadding (batting) 4½in (11.5cm) square
- Polyester toy filling
- Red and green embroidery cotton (floss)

For scissor keep

- Scraps of red spotty fabric and green fabric
- Scraps of white, blue floral and candy striped fabric
- Polyester toy filling
- Red and white baker's twine
- Red and green embroidery cotton (floss)

FINISHED SIZES

Pincushion 4¼in (11cm) square approx.
Scissor keep 2in x 1¾in (5cm x 4.5cm) approx.
Use ¼in (5mm) seam allowances unless otherwise stated

PIECING THE PINCUSHION

1. Trace the square template onto thin card and cut out. Use the template to cut nine squares from scrap paper. Cut four squares in half to make triangles.

2. Using the card template, cut out four blue fabric squares ¼in (5mm) larger all round than the template. In the same way cut out one white square, four white triangles and four striped triangles. Place a paper template in the middle of a fabric shape, wrong side up, and fold the fabric edges over the paper and tack (baste) in place. Repeat for all the fabric shapes.

3. Join the patchwork pieces together in rows as in Fig 1. Sew the rows together. When all the patchwork is complete, remove the paper and press.

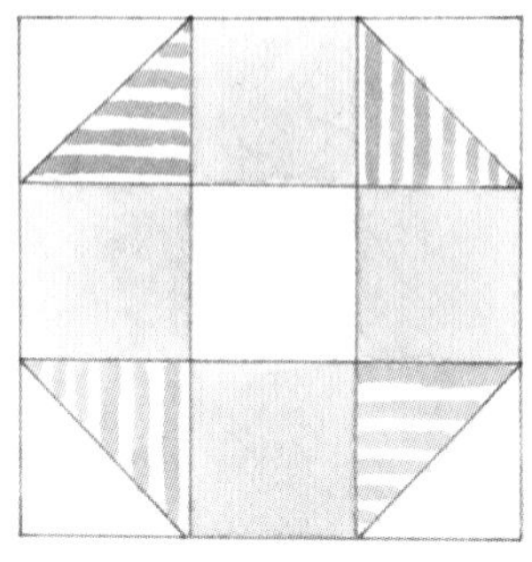

Fig 1

ADDING THE APPLIQUÉ

4. Iron fusible web onto red spotty fabric and green fabric. Using the template, trace the small strawberry onto the back of the red fabric. Trace three leaves onto the back of the green fabric. Cut the shapes out and arrange on the centre square. Peel off the backing and iron in place (Fig 2).

Fig 2

5. Stitch around the strawberry with red embroidery cotton (floss) and blanket stitch. Stitch around the leaves with green and blanket stitch (see Basic Techniques: Stitches).

MAKING UP THE PINCUSHION

6. Place wadding (batting) behind the patchwork. Quilt round the centre square with red embroidery cotton (floss) and round the corner square and triangles with white.

7. Cut a 4½in (11.5cm) square from pink/white striped fabric for backing. With right sides together, sew round the pincushion, leaving a gap on one side. Trim seams, clip corners and turn right way out, pushing out the corners. Stuff with filling and sew the gap closed.

MAKING THE SCISSOR KEEP

8. Cut one 2½in (6.5cm) square from blue floral, one from white and one from pink stripe. Cut the pink/white striped fabric squares in half, sew together down the long side and press (Fig 3).

Fig 3

9. Iron fusible web onto a scrap of red spotty fabric and a scrap of green fabric. Using the template, trace the large strawberry onto the back of the red spotty fabric and the green stalk and leaves onto the back of the green fabric. Cut them out.

10. Place the fruit and leaves as shown (Fig 4). Peel off the paper and iron in place. Use red embroidery cotton (floss) to blanket stitch the strawberry and then green for the leaves.

Fig 4

11. Make up in the same way as the pincushion using the blue floral backing square. Use red embroidery cotton (floss) to work running stitches around the edge. Thread a large-eyed needle with twine, push it through one corner and tie in a knot.

Templates (full size)

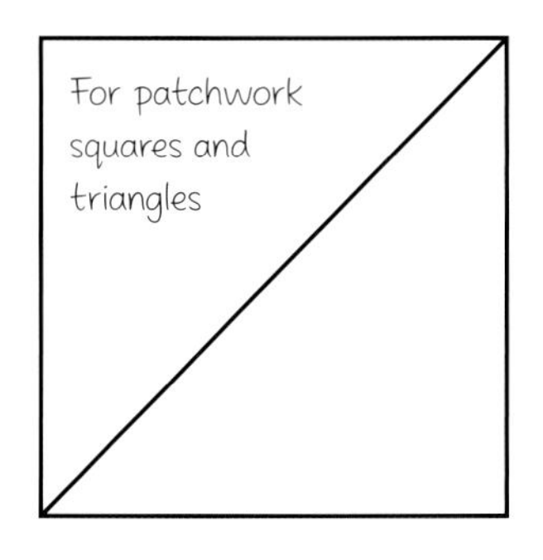

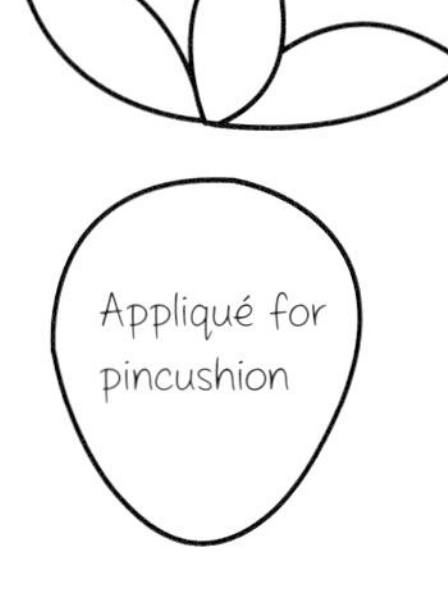

STAR QUILT

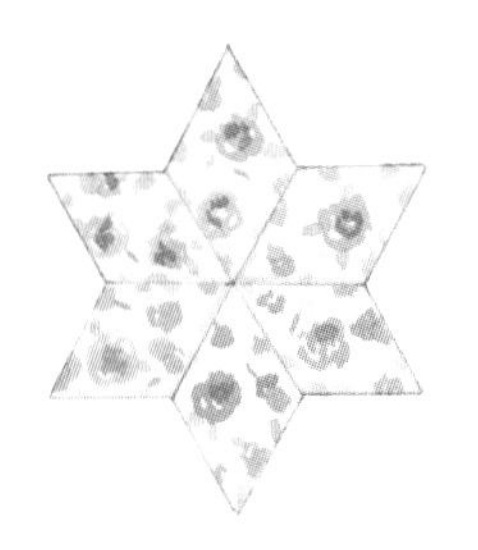

This beautiful quilt is not only fun to make but is also a starry stash buster. Each star is made from six English paper pieced diamonds, joined together with plain white hexagons. The diamond paper pieces make the star shapes sharp and accurate and simple to sew together, and the whole effect is lively and colourful. To save time you can buy ready-cut diamond and hexagon templates – see Tip.

You will need

- Pre-cut diamond paper pieces (264) with 2in (5cm) sides (see Tip and templates)
- Pre-cut hexagon paper pieces (88) with 2in (5cm) sides (see Tip and templates)
- Scrap fabrics in various colours, about 8in (20cm) square is needed for each star shape (there are forty-four stars in total)
- White fabric for background and border 2yd (1.75m)
- Polka dot fabric for backing 1½yd (1.5m) if using 60in (150cm) wide
- Wadding (batting) 50in x 58in (125cm x 150cm) approx
- Pink/white striped fabric for binding ½yd (0.5m)
- Sewing threads to suit fabrics

FINISHED SIZE

45½in x 53½in (115.5cm x 135cm) approx.
Use ¼in (5mm) seams unless otherwise stated.

PREPARING THE TEMPLATES

1. Use the templates provided. Template A is the diamond for the stars and Template B is the hexagon needed to join with the pieced stars – you may decide to buy these templates ready-cut. Templates C, D, E, F and G are needed for straightening the sides of the quilt. You will need to copy and then cut the following paper templates.

- Template A (diamond) – you will need 264 (six each for forty-four stars).
- Template B (hexagon) – you will need eighty-eight.
- Template C – cut six. Note that half the template is given, so follow the template instructions to make the complete shape.
- Template D – cut two. If using a print fabric, cut one shape as a reversed version.
- Template E – cut eleven.
- Template F – cut two. If using a print fabric, cut one shape as a reversed version.
- Template G – cut eight.
- Template H – cut two.

tip

You can buy packs of ready-cut paper pieces in all sorts of shapes and sizes, including diamonds and hexagons. Check out your local quilt store, online, or see Suppliers. For this quilt you will need a diamond shape with 2in (5cm) sides and a hexagon with 2in (5cm) sides. You can re-use the templates if you like. The diamond and hexagon shapes are also provided as templates.

MAKING THE STARS

2. To make the stars use an English paper piecing method. To make one star, cut out six diamond shapes from fabric ¼in (5mm) bigger all round than the paper template. Fold a fabric diamond carefully around a paper diamond and tack (baste) in place (Fig 1). Press firmly. Repeat with the other diamonds.

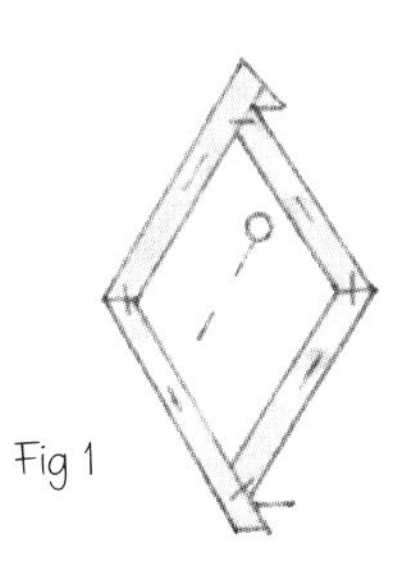
Fig 1

3. Sew together three diamonds using white thread and whip stitch (Fig 2). Sew together a second set of three diamonds. Now join the two sets together along the straight centre edge. Press the finished star well. Make forty-four stars in total.

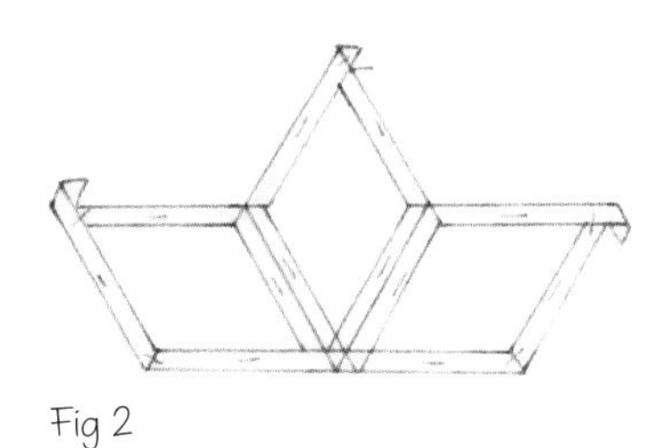
Fig 2

4. Cut out eighty-eight hexagons from white fabric, ¼in (5mm) bigger all round than the hexagon paper shape. Tack (baste) the fabric round the hexagons in the same way as the diamonds.

tip

Cutting the diamond shapes from fabric will be faster if you create a template ¼in (5mm) bigger all round than the paper diamond and mark the shape repeatedly all along a 1½in (4.4cm) wide x width of fabric strip. You could also use the 30-degree angle on your rotary cutter.

ASSEMBLING THE QUILT

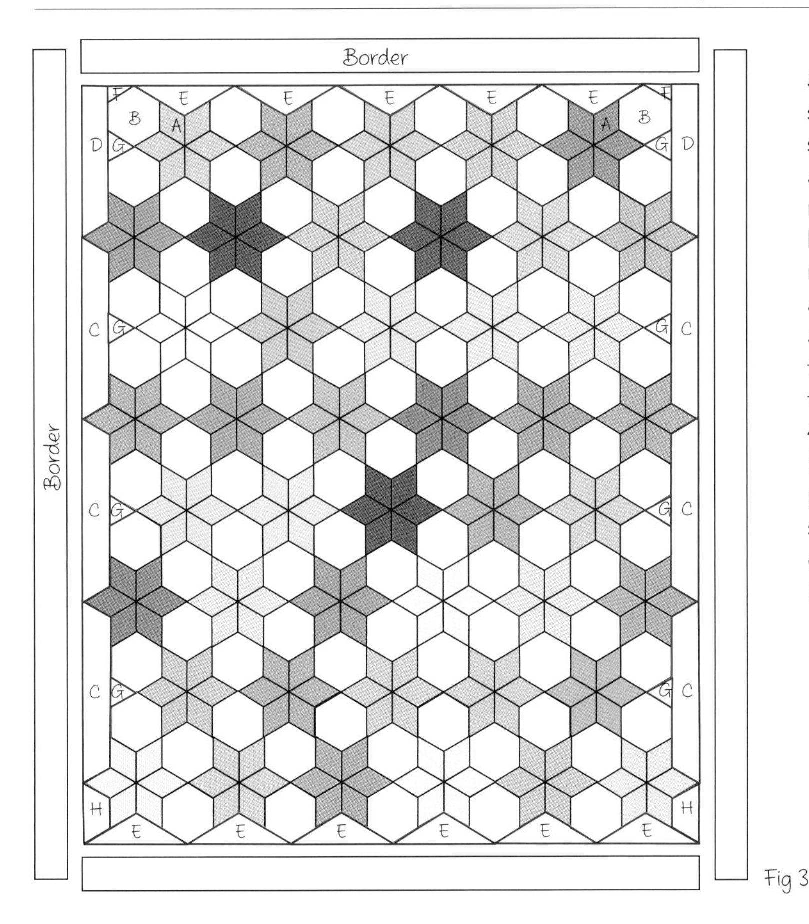

Fig 3

5. Lay out the stars on a flat surface, starting with a row of five stars, then a row of six stars, and alternating until you have eight rows – see Fig 3. Place the hexagons between the stars and move the stars around until you are happy with the colour arrangement. Now begin to join the pieces together, whip stitching the edges together, as before (Fig 4). When all of the diamonds and hexagons are joined, remove the paper templates from the centre section – leave those around the edges in place for the moment. Press the patchwork.

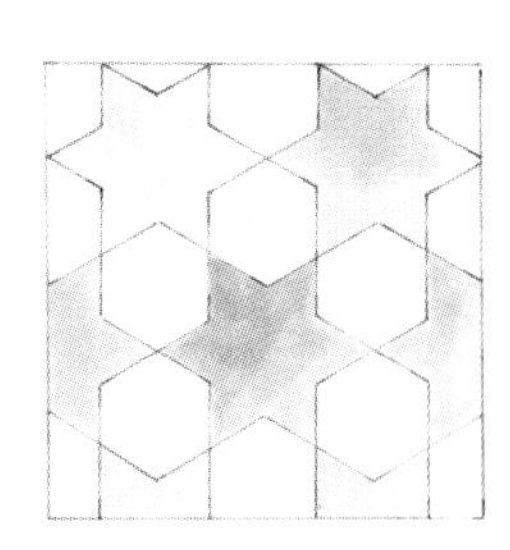
Fig 4

6. To fill in the sides of the quilt and straighten up the edges, use the C to H paper templates (shown in red on Fig 3). Cut fabric shapes ¼in (5mm) larger all round than the paper templates and tack (baste) these to the paper templates, as before. Referring to Fig 3 and Fig 5A and 5B for detail, add these shapes to the quilt, sewing them in place to fill in the sides and corners. Remove all of the paper templates. Press well and check that the quilt has straight sides and right-angled corners, trimming if needs be.

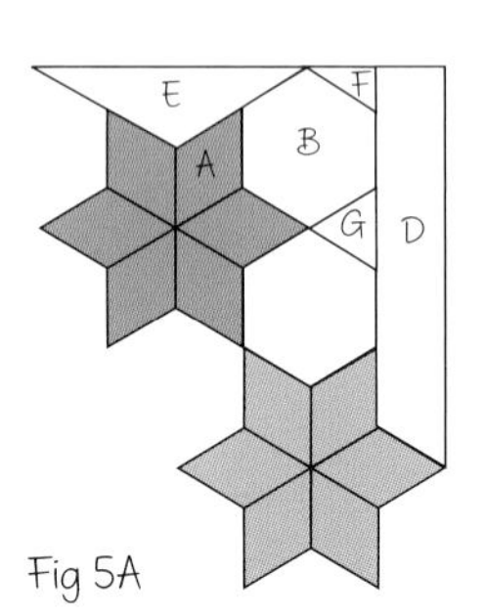

Fig 5A

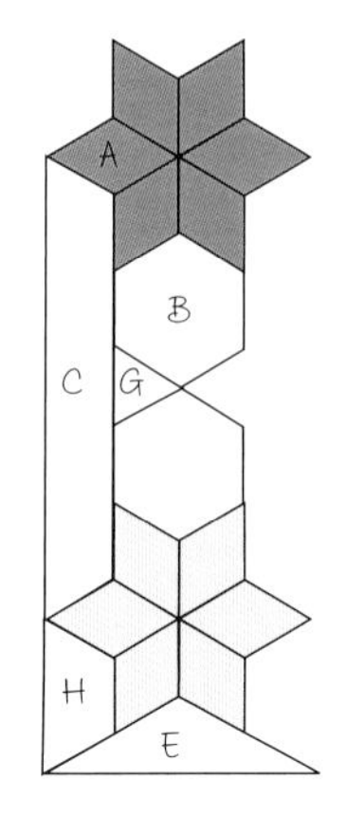

Fig 5B

ADDING THE BORDER

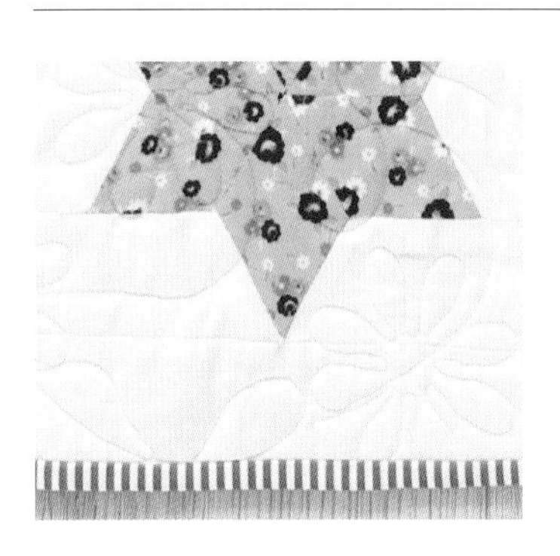

7. Lay your quilt out flat and measure the width, making a note of this measurement. Cut two 2½in (6.5cm) wide strips of white fabric to this measurement and sew these along the top and bottom of the quilt. Press the seams outwards. Now measure the length of the quilt (including the two borders you just added) and cut two strips to this measurement – you will need to join strips together to make the correct length. Sew these to the sides of the quilt and press the seams outwards.

QUILTING AND FINISHING

8. Prepare a quilt sandwich of the backing, wadding (batting) and patchwork (see Basic Techniques: Making a Quilt Sandwich).

9. Quilt as desired by hand or machine. My quilt was long-arm quilted with a daisy pattern. When quilting is finished, tidy all thread ends and square up your quilt by trimming the backing and wadding (batting) level with the edges of the quilt all round.

10. Prepare the binding by cutting six strips 2½in (6.5cm) x width of fabric from pink/white striped fabric (cutting so the stripe will appear vertical when the binding is sewn). Join the strips together and press seams open. Press the binding in half, wrong sides together, all along the length and bind your quilt – see Basic Techniques: Binding.

Templates (full size)

All of the templates are cut from paper. When cutting out the fabric shapes, add ¼in (5mm) seam allowance all around before cutting out.

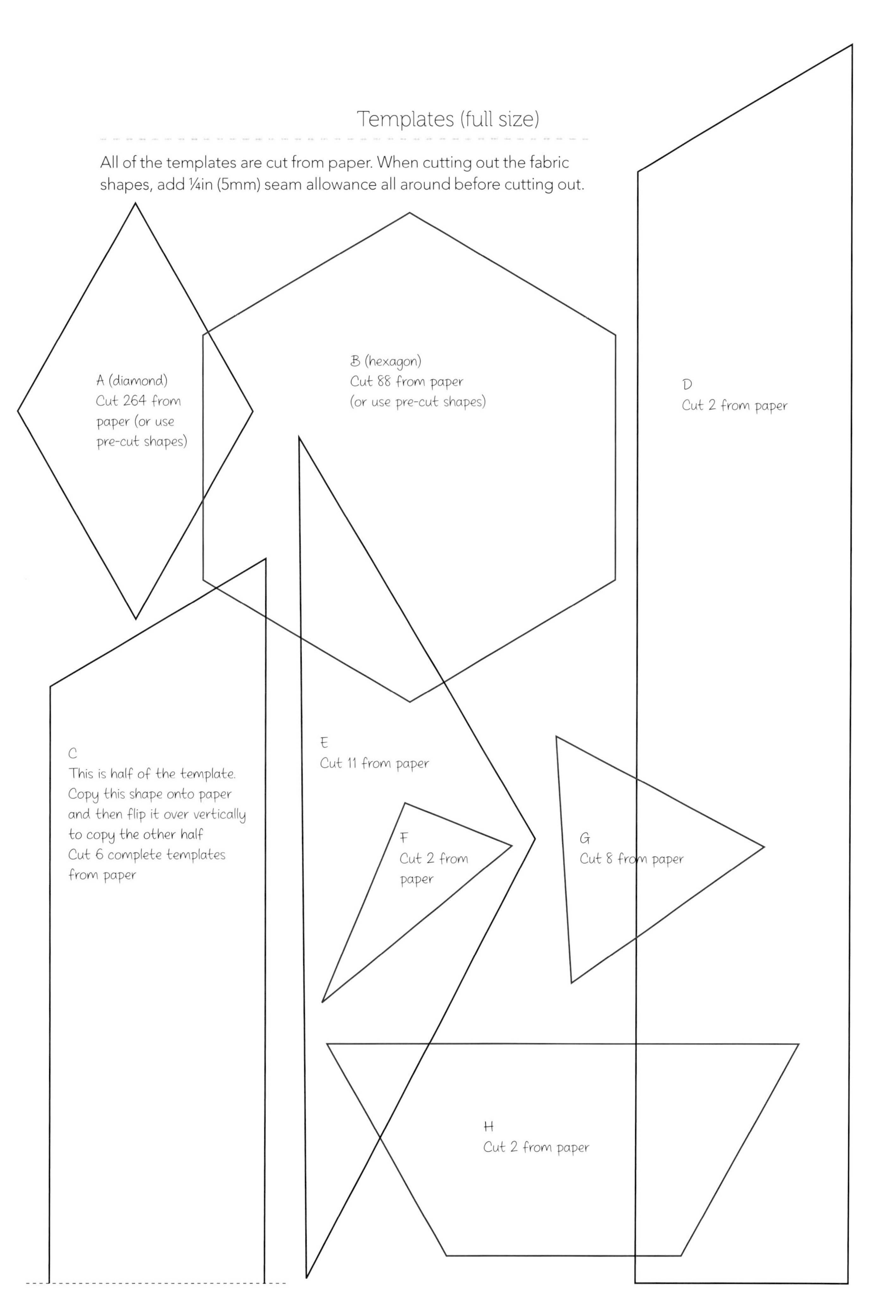

PATCHWORK FLOWER BUCKET

Hexagons are a traditional patchwork shape and are always fun to make and use. This patchwork project uses hexagons and fabric flowers with button centres to make a special little storage bucket, perfect as a gift filled with treats. There is also a simpler, matching drawstring bag to make when time is short – see the Hexagon Drawstring Bag project. Both bags use the English paper piecing method for the patchwork.

For the bucket

- Thin card for template
- Scrap paper
- Scraps of floral fabric
- Coordinating fabric 10in x 6½in (25.5cm x 16.5cm)
- Striped lining fabric two pieces 6½in x 10in (16.5 x 25.5cm)
- Lace for trim, about 1in x 14in (2.5cm x 35.5cm)
- Lightweight fusible wadding (batting) two pieces 6½in x 10in (16.5 x 25.5cm)
- White sewing thread

For the flowers

- Scraps of floral fabrics
- Felt scraps
- Two buttons
- Glue gun (optional)

XXXXXXXXXXXXXXXXXXXXXXX

FINISHED SIZE

6in x 8in (15cm x 20cm) approx. (with top folded down)
Use ¼in (5mm) seam allowances unless otherwise stated

PIECING THE PATCHWORK

1. Trace the hexagon template provided onto thin card and cut it out. Draw around the template onto scrap paper forty times and cut out the shapes. Use the card template to cut out forty fabric scraps, cutting out the shapes ¼in (5mm) larger all round.

2. Place a paper template in the middle of a fabric shape, wrong side up, and fold the fabric edges over the paper neatly and tack (baste) in place. Repeat for all the fabric shapes.

3. Lay out twenty fabric-covered hexagons in a nice arrangement for the front of the bag (in five columns each with four hexagons). Sew them together by placing the hexagons right sides together and whip stitching the seams. Once complete, trim the patchwork to 6½in (16.5cm) wide x 7½in (19cm) high. Repeat this process to create the bag back from the remaining twenty hexagons.

4. Cut two 3in x 6½in (7.5cm x 16.5cm) pieces of coordinating fabric. Sew one piece to the bottom of the front hexagon patchwork, and one to the bottom of the back patchwork. Each piece of patchwork should now be about 10in x 6½in (25.5cm x 16.5cm) (Fig. 1).

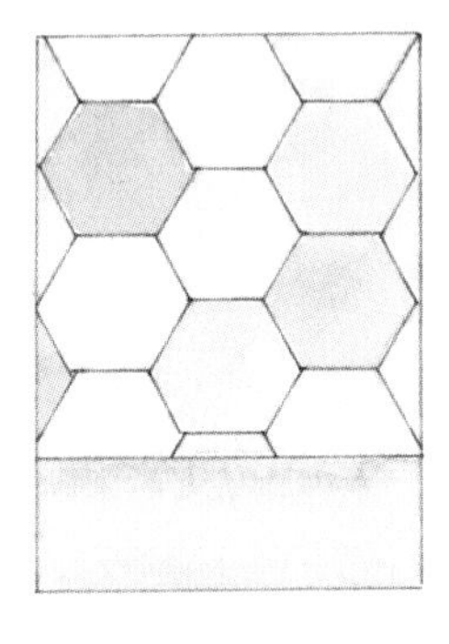

Fig 1

5. Cut two lengths of lace to fit the width of the patchwork and slipstitch one in place just above the join on the front patchwork and one on the back.

ASSEMBLING THE BAG OUTER

6. Iron a piece of fusible wadding (batting) to the wrong side of the bag front and back. Place the front and back of the bag right sides together and sew together along the sides and bottom. To create depth to the bag, fold the bottom corners as shown in Fig 2, machine sew across the corners and trim excess fabric.

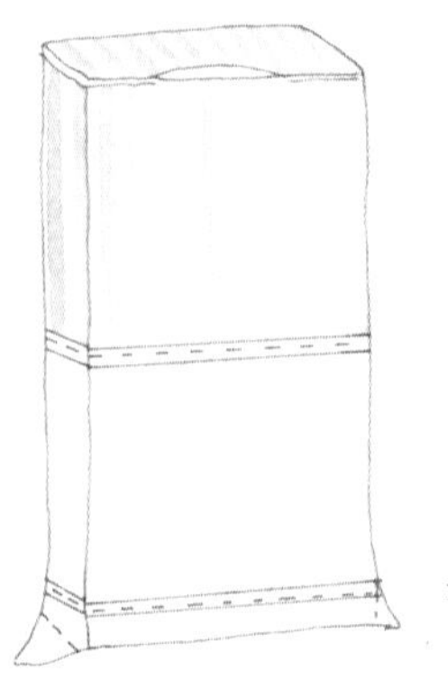

Fig 2

MAKING THE LINING

7. Using the two pieces of striped lining fabric, make a lining bag in the same way as the bag outer, but leave a small opening in the bottom for turning through.

8. Turn the bag inside out and place the lining inside, so right sides are together. Sew round the top edge of the bag and lining. Pull the bag and lining out through the gap. Push the lining back into the bag and smooth out. Press the bag carefully and topstitch round the top edge. Fold the top of the bag down to show the striped lining.

tip

This little bucket is perfect for adding pretty embellishments. I used fabric flowers but you could use buttons, beads, bows, tags or other decorations of your choice.

MAKING THE FLOWERS

9. Cut out three 3in (7.5cm) diameter circles from floral fabric. Cut each circle in half. Fold five of the semi-circles in half and sew along the straight edge (Fig 3). Turn right side out and press. Using white sewing thread, sew along the curved edge, pull to gather and fasten off (Fig 4).

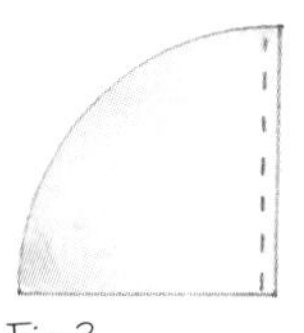

Fig 3

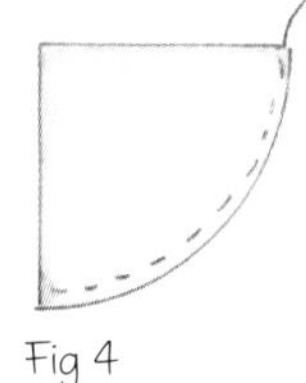

Fig 4

10. Join the petals together by sewing them one by one onto a long piece of thread through the centre gathered edges (Fig 5). Pull the thread tight and finish off securely. Cut a small circle of felt and glue or sew it to the back of the flower to secure the petals together. Finish by gluing or sewing a button to the flower centre. Make another flower like this. Glue or sew a flower to either side of the bag to finish (Fig 6).

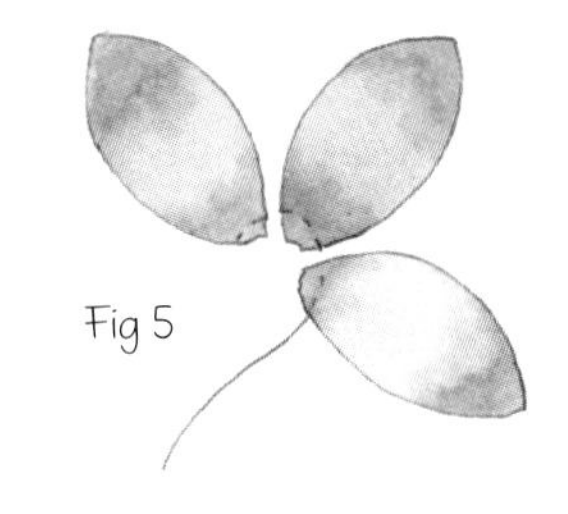

Fig 5

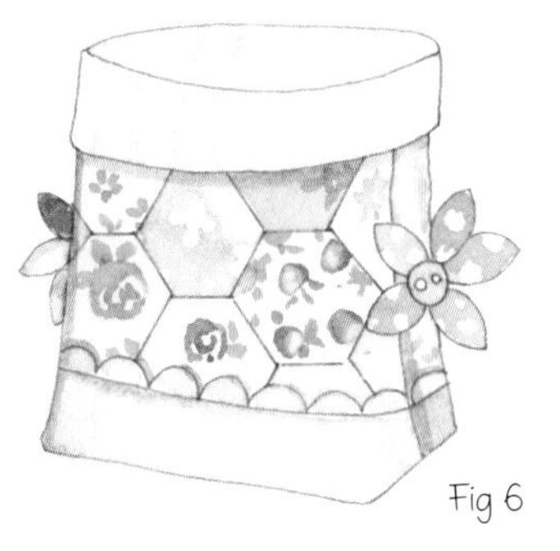

Fig 6

Template (full size)

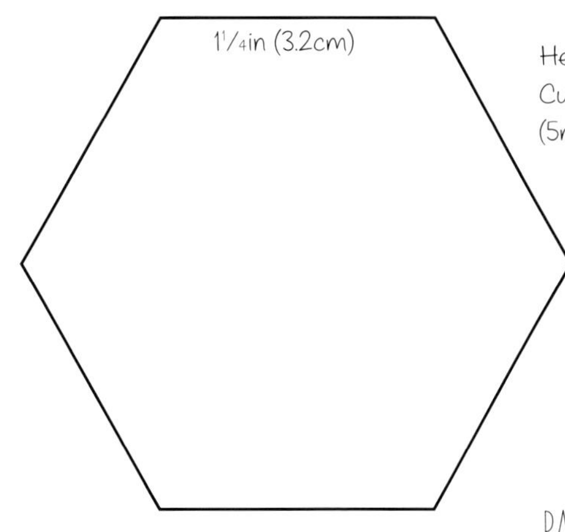

Hexagon for paper template
Cut out fabric patches ¼in (5mm) larger all round

STAR PINCUSHION

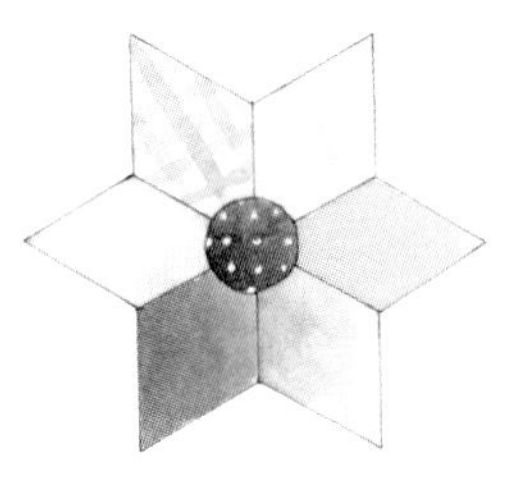

This little pincushion is so colourful and is a pleasure to make. Small pincushions like this make perfect gifts and are sure to please any stitching or crafting friend – we always need a new pincushion and can never have too many! It's also a great way to use up small scraps of favourite fabrics, and the pattern and colour combinations are endless and fun to discover. You can also add pretty buttons to finish it off nicely.

REVERSE
24
SPECIAL SILK FINISH
THREAD
SYLKO
36
MACHINE
TWIST

You will need

- Twelve 2in (5cm) diamond paper pieces (the measurement refers to each side of the diamond)
- Assorted cotton fabric scraps
- Polyester toy filling
- Red spotted button and red plain button
- White sewing thread

FINISHED SIZE

6in x 7in (15cm x 18cm) approx.
Use a ¼in (5mm) seam allowance unless otherwise stated

PIECING THE PINCUSHION

1. Trace the diamond template onto thin card and cut out. Using scrap paper, draw the diamond shape twelve times in total and cut out the shapes accurately.

2. Choose the fabrics you wish to use and cut out twelve fabric diamonds ¼in (5mm) bigger all round than the paper diamond shape. Fold the fabric carefully around each paper shape and tack (baste) in place neatly (Fig 1). Repeat to create twelve fabric diamonds.

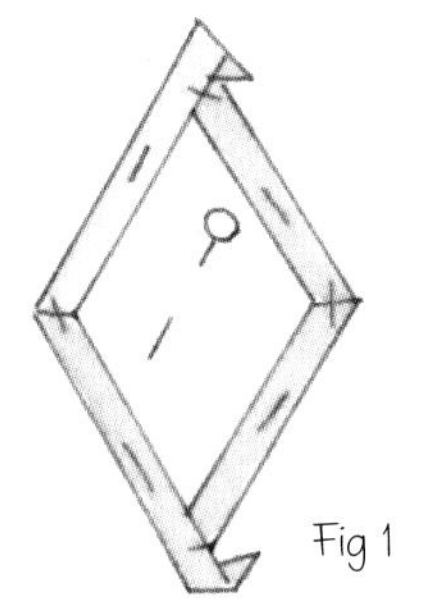
Fig 1

3. When you have made the six diamonds for the front and six for the back of the star, begin sewing the diamonds together as follows. Place two diamonds right sides together and sew together, using whip stitch and white cotton thread. It is best to sew the diamonds in two groups of three and then join the long centre seam across the centre (Fig 2). Working in this way prevents a small hole from forming in the centre of the star and creates a stronger shape. When the back and the front of the star are completed, remove the papers and press carefully.

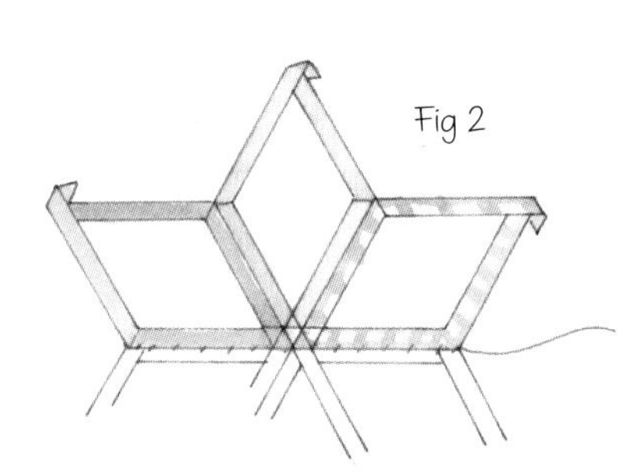
Fig 2

MAKING UP

4. Pin the front and back of the star right sides together and whip stitch together, stopping at the last two diamond edges (Fig 3). Remove the pins and turn the star out to the right side. Stuff the star firmly and then sew the last two edges neatly.

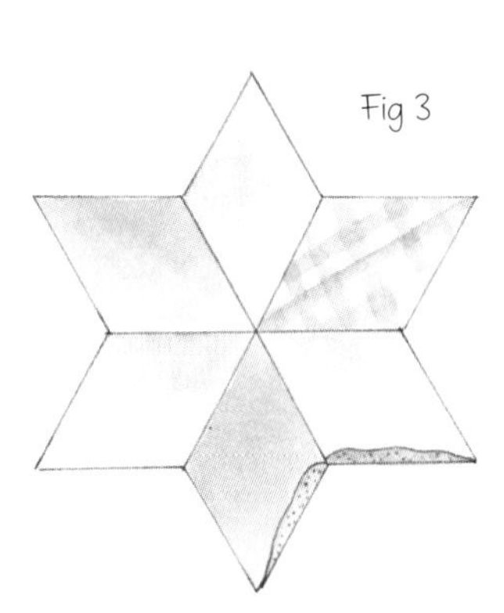

Fig 3

5. To finish, sew a spotty button on the centre front of the star and a plain red button on the centre back (Fig 4).

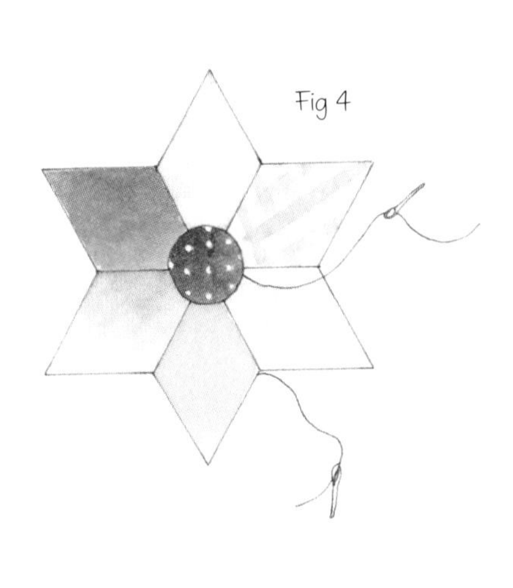

Fig 4

Template (full size)

Diamond for paper template
Cut out fabric patches 1/4in (5mm) larger all round

2in (5cm)

RED, WHITE & BLUE STAR QUILT

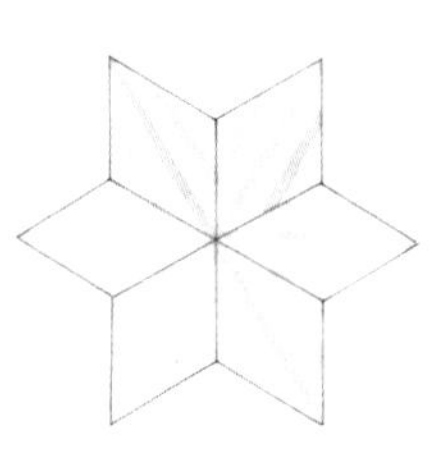

This little quilt uses one of my favourite colour combinations. I have always loved the fresh, nautical shades of red, white and blue, as they remind me of seaside holidays as a child and of flags and bunting flying in the coastal breezes. This little starry quilt is easy and fun to make using English paper piecing and appliqué. You can use striped fabric for the diamonds that make up the pieced stars and enjoy playing with the effects the stripes create.

You will need

- Red striped and blue striped fabric for large stars, about ⅛yd (0.125cm) of each
- Red spotty fabric for one medium star, about 4in (10cm) square
- Blue striped fabric for four small stars, about 6in (15cm) square
- White fabric for background and border ⅜yd (0.35m)
- White fabric for backing 20in (50cm) square
- Fusible web
- Thin card for template
- Scrap paper
- Sewing threads to match fabrics
- Wadding (batting) 20in (50cm) square
- Striped red/white/blue fabric for binding ¼yd (0.25m)

FINISHED SIZE

18in (45cm) square approx. Use ¼in (5mm) seam allowances unless otherwise stated

MAKING THE LARGE STARS

1. There are four large stars, each made with six diamonds. Prepare twenty-four paper diamonds – for the method see Basic Techniques: English Paper Piecing. To make one star, prepare six fabric diamonds (Fig 1), whip stitch them together (Fig 2) and press. Make two red stars like this and two blue.

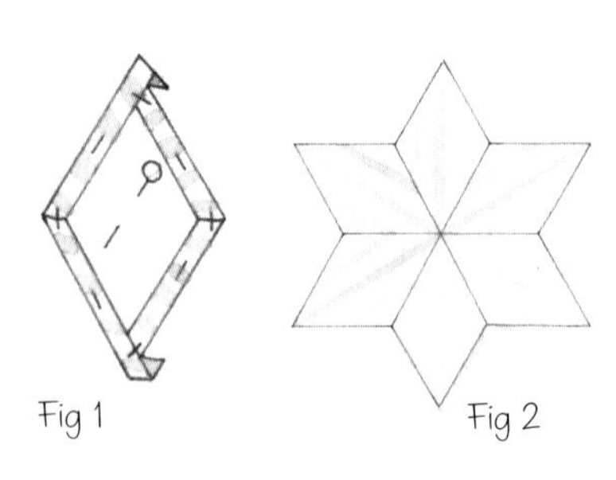

Fig 1 Fig 2

tip

You can create a radiating pattern with striped fabric if you place the template so that the stripes run vertically through each diamond.

ADDING THE BACKGROUND

2. For the backgrounds to the large stars, use the same process to cut out forty paper diamonds. Cover these with white fabric. Join the large stars together with white diamonds, as in Fig 3.

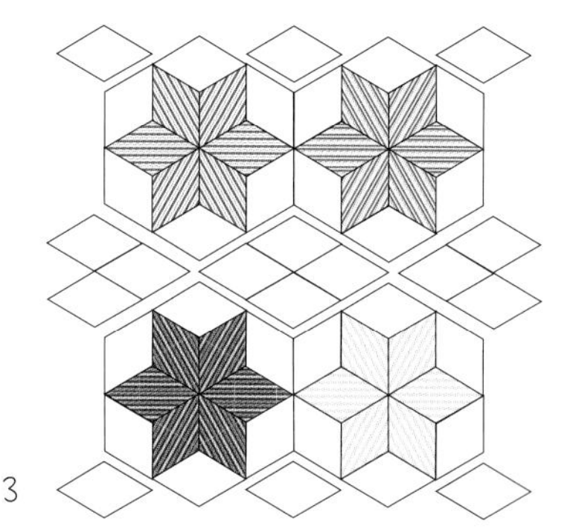

Fig 3

MAKING THE APPLIQUÉ STARS

3. There are five appliqué stars in the quilt – one medium red and four small blue. Cut one 4in (10cm) square of red fabric and one 6in (15cm) square of blue and back them with fusible web. Trace the small and medium templates onto thin card and cut out. Draw round the small star template onto the paper side of the fusible web four times and the medium star once. Cut out the stars carefully.

4. Position the stars on the quilt, peel off the backing and iron in place. Edge the stars with red thread and blanket stitch.

5. Trim the quilt top to about 14in (35.5cm) square (Fig 4), or ¼in (5mm) beyond the outer point of each large star (to allow for a seam).

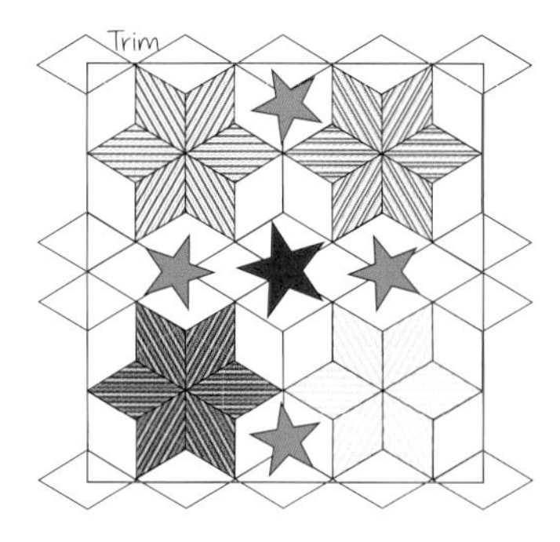

Fig 4

ADDING THE BORDER

6. From white fabric cut two border strips 2½in x 14in (6.5cm x 35.5cm) and two strips 2½in x 18½in (6.5cm x 45cm). If your quilt measurements differ from mine, then cut the border strips long enough to fit *your* quilt. Sew the shorter strips to the top and bottom of the quilt and press seams outwards. Sew the longer strips to the sides of the quilt and press seams outwards.

QUILTING AND FINISHING

7. Prepare for quilting (see Basic Techniques: Making a Quilt Sandwich). Quilt as desired. This quilt was machine quilted with a small stipple design around the stars and white background.

8. Trim excess wadding (batting) and backing and square up. For the binding, if you are using striped fabric cut sufficient strips with the stripes *diagonally* to make a length of about 80in (205cm) once sewn together. Press seams open. Use this to bind the quilt – see Basic Techniques: Binding.

Templates (full size)

Use the diamond to make paper templates for the large English paper-pieced stars
Cut out fabric patches ¼in (5mm) larger all round

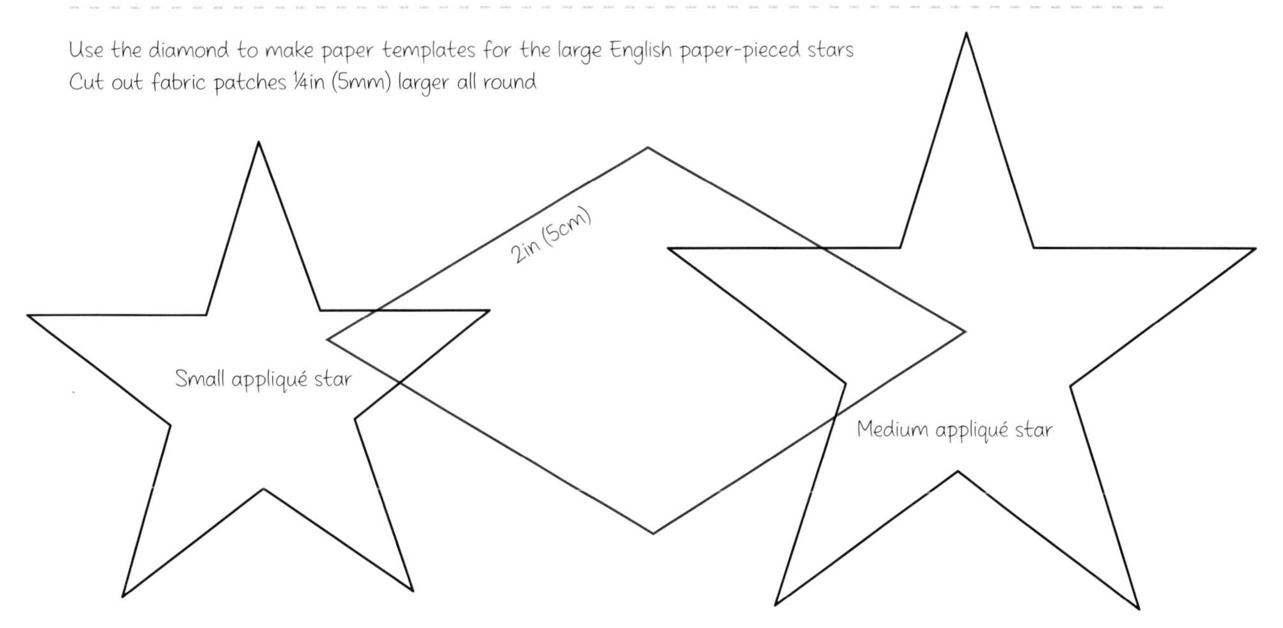

SWEET DOLL

I always enjoy making fabric toys. They are a sewing tradition going back centuries and are so simple and satisfying to create. Making this little doll was fun, and when I drew on her little face I thought she looked so sweet. Her dress is made from two coordinating prints with a little lace trimming and a ribbon sash. You can have fun choosing your doll's dress fabric from your own stash and adding any lace or ribbon embellishments you like. You can also choose different coloured yarn for her hair if you wish, making her unique.

You will need

- Thin card for templates
- Pink cotton fabric for doll body ½yd (0.5m)
- Polyester toy filling
- Light brown wool yarn for hair
- Tissue paper
- Double-sided adhesive tape
- Two different, coordinating floral fabrics for dress bodice and skirt, about 9in x 11in (25cm x 28cm) of each
- Sewing threads to suit fabrics
- Blue ribbon ¼in (5mm) wide x about 18in (45cm) long
- White lace ⅝in (1.5cm) wide x about 18in (45cm) long
- Fine fabric marker in black and blusher for features
- Fabric glue
- Small button for back bodice

XXXXXXXXXXXXXXXXXXXXXXX

FINISHED SIZE

13in (35cm) tall approx.
Use ¼in (5mm) seam allowances unless otherwise stated

MAKING THE DOLL

1. Trace the patterns for the doll's body and head, the arm and the leg onto thin card and cut out to make templates.

2. Fold the pink fabric in half and lay the templates on top. Trace round the head and body templates and then trace the arm and leg templates twice. Sew round the shapes before cutting out. Sew round the head and body leaving a gap at the dotted lines. Sew round the arms and legs in the same way.

3. Cut out the shapes and turn the right way out, easing out the points of the limbs. Stuff the head and body. Gather the head at the neck with running stitch and insert into the top of the body, sewing in place by hand (Fig 1). Stuff the arms and legs. Insert the legs into the base of the body and sew across the seam (Fig 2). Sew the arms closed and then sew them to either side of the body (Fig 3).

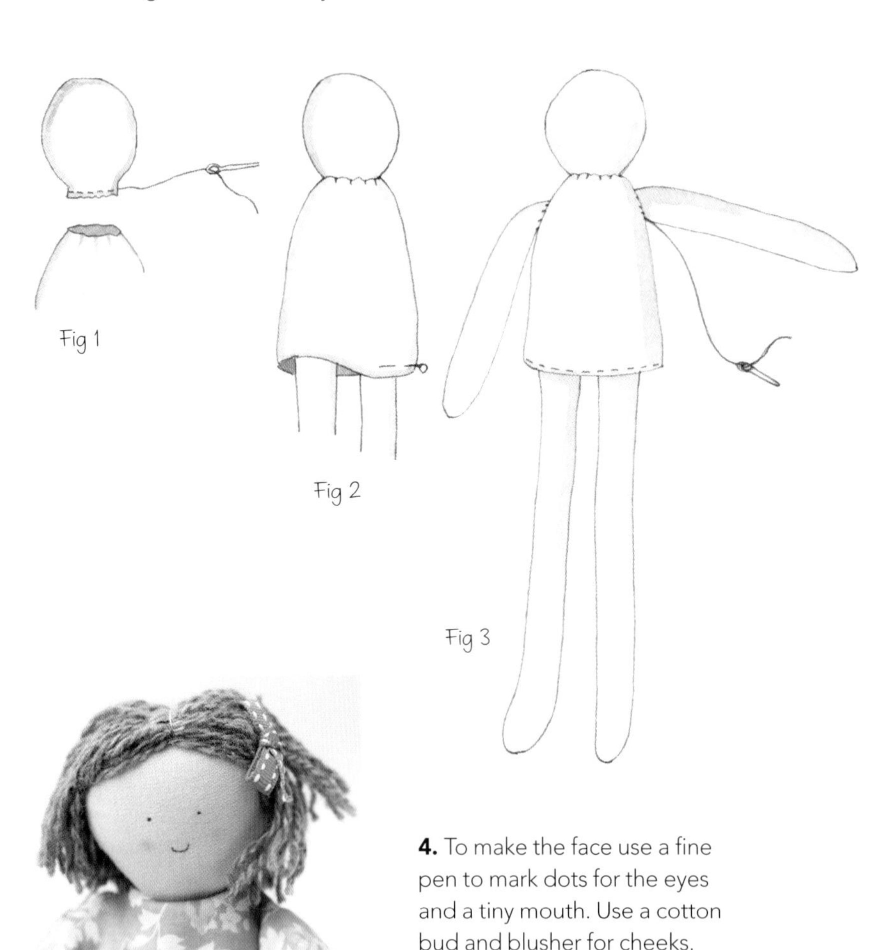

4. To make the face use a fine pen to mark dots for the eyes and a tiny mouth. Use a cotton bud and blusher for cheeks.

MAKING THE HAIR

5. The hair is like a tiny wig. Take a piece of tissue paper 6¾in x 3½in (17cm x 9cm) and lay strips of double-sided tape across it so the paper is covered (Fig 4). Peel off the second layer to leave the sticky side exposed. Cut lengths of brown yarn about 7in (18cm) long, and enough to cover the tissue with no gaps (Fig 5). Lay in place on the tissue backing and press down firmly. Find the centre of the hair and sew along it to form a parting (Fig 6). When securely sewn, trim to length, or leave choppy if you prefer. Peel away the tissue paper and tape until just the yarn hair remains.

6. Place the hair on the head and add a little fabric glue and a few stitches to keep it in place. Add more yarn strands to fill in at the back if needed (Fig 7).

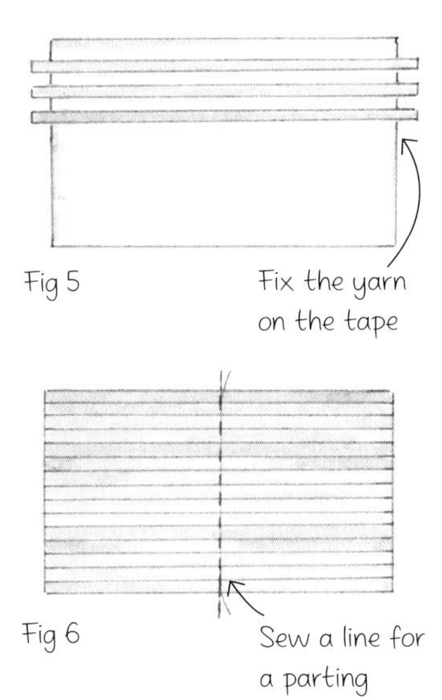

Fig 4 Put double-sided tape on tissue paper

MAKING THE DRESS

7. Trace the bodice and sleeve templates onto thin card and cut them out. Take the bodice fabric and draw round the pattern for the front and back pieces (cutting one back piece as a reversed piece). Place the sleeve pattern on folded fabric and draw round it. Repeat to make the second sleeve. Cut out the pieces.

8. Place the back and front pieces of the bodice together and join at the shoulder seams. Sew up the side seams. Sew up the sleeve seams and then insert them into the bodice and stitch in place. Turn a tiny hem down the back opening and along the neck edge and stitch neatly by hand.

9. Cut a piece of skirt fabric 6¼in x 14½in (16cm x 40cm). Sew a small hem along the bottom. Gather the skirt top into several pleats so it matches the size of the bodice. Pin and then tack (baste) the pleats in place. Sew the skirt to the bodice and then remove the tacking stitches. Sew up the back seam of the skirt. Sew a button to the top of the bodice at the back to finish.

10. Hand sew the lace trim to the bottom of the dress and to the cuffs of the sleeves. Put the dress on the doll and tie a ribbon sash round the waist, making a bow at the back. Make a tiny matching bow for the doll's hair.

Templates (full size)

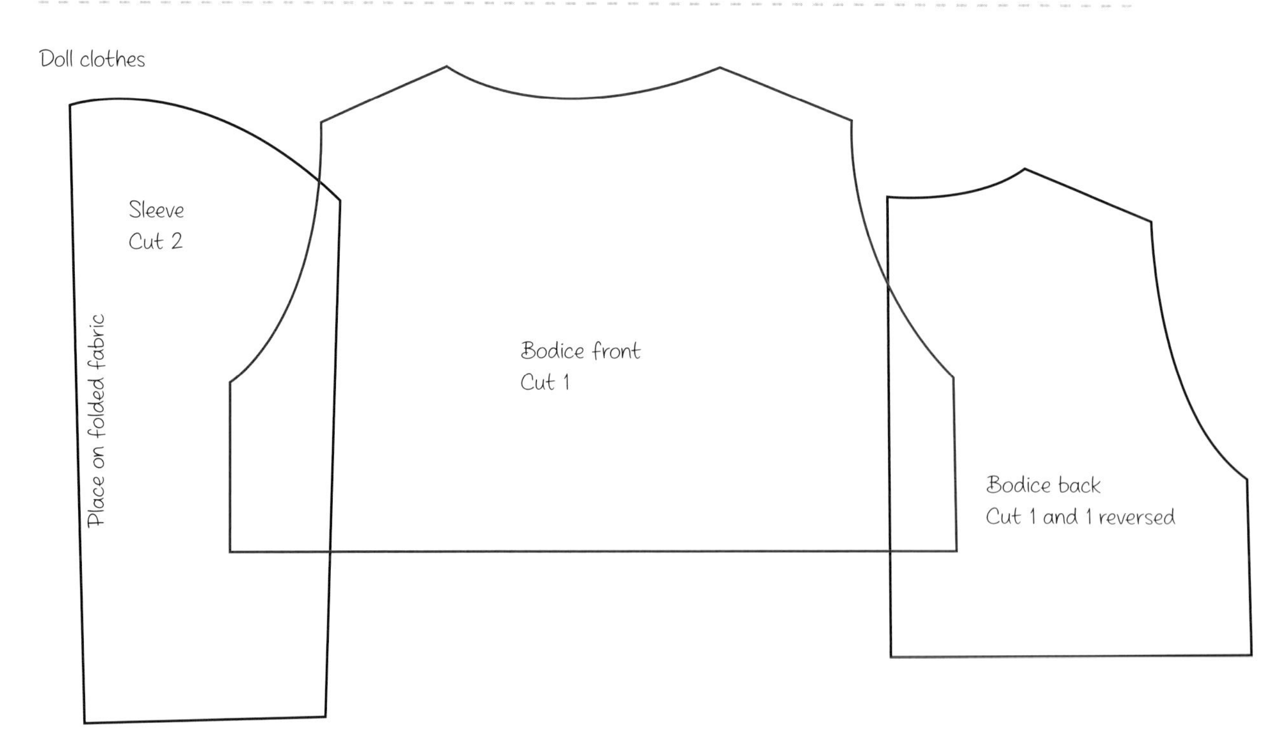

Templates (full size)

Doll body

These templates are also used for the Christmas Angel

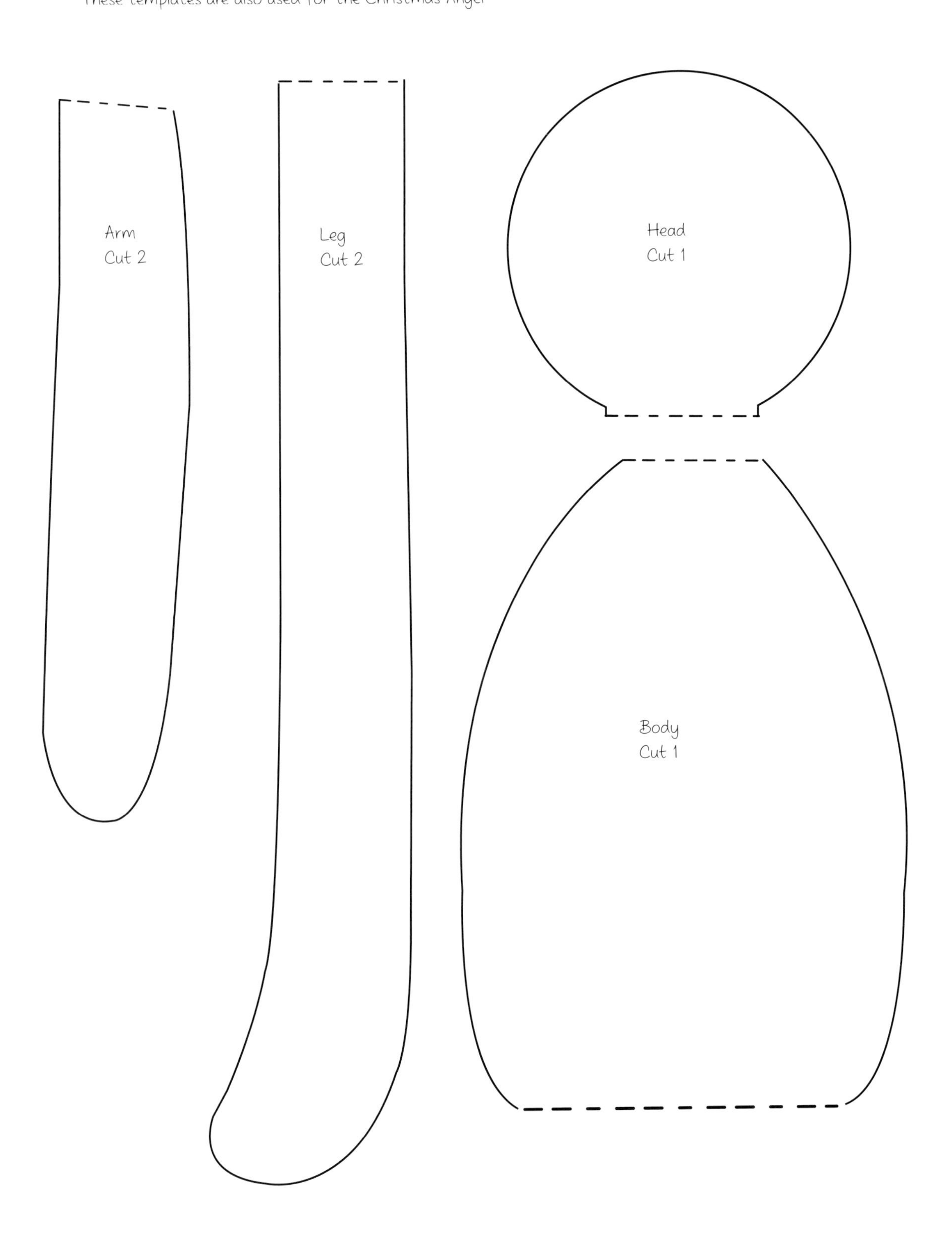

MUSHROOM PILLOW

Mushrooms and toadstools are definitely among my favourite decorative motifs for autumn crafting. The dotty fabrics in this little decorative pillow echo the cute spotted appliqué toadstool in the centre. This little pillow is a companion to the Pumpkin Pillow and they would look very pretty given together as a gift for autumn.

seam
-noun
1. the line formed
ap·pli·qué
-noun
1. ornamentation,
decorative feature,
technique in which
patches are layered
foundation fabric,
stitched in place by
or machine with the

You will need

- Blue spotted fabric for pillow centre 5¼in (13.5cm) square
- Red spotted fabric for appliqué 3¼in x 2¼in (8.5cm x 6cm)
- Scrap of plain white fabric
- Text print fabric for border 2½in x 5¼in (6.5cm x 13.5cm)
- Red spotted floral fabric for border 2¼in x 7¼in (6cm x 18.5cm)
- Polka dot fabric for border 2¼in x 7¼in (4.5cm x 18.5cm)
- Grey floral spot fabric for border 2½in x 8¾in (6.5cm x 23.5cm)
- Thin card for templates
- Fusible web
- White sewing thread and red embroidery cotton (floss)
- Red polka dot button
- Thin wadding (batting) 9½in x 7½in (14cm x 19cm)
- Cream patterned backing fabric 10in x 9in (25.5cm x 23cm)
- Cushion pad 9in x 8in (23cm x 20.5cm) – make your own (see Basic Techniques)

FINISHED SIZE

9½in x 8½in (24cm x 21.5cm) approx.
Use ¼in (5mm) seam allowances unless otherwise stated

MAKING THE APPLIQUÉ

1. Using the templates, trace the cap and stalk onto thin card and cut out. Iron fusible web onto the back of the red spotted fabric and the plain white scrap. Place the cap template on the back of the red spotted fabric, draw round the shape carefully and cut it out (Fig 1). Draw round the stalk onto the back of the white fabric and cut it out.

2. Take the piece of blue spotted fabric for the pillow centre and position the mushroom centrally on it, with the cap overlapping the stalk. Peel off the fusible web backing and iron in place (Fig 2). Sew round the mushroom cap with red embroidery cotton (floss) and blanket stitch and the stalk with white thread.

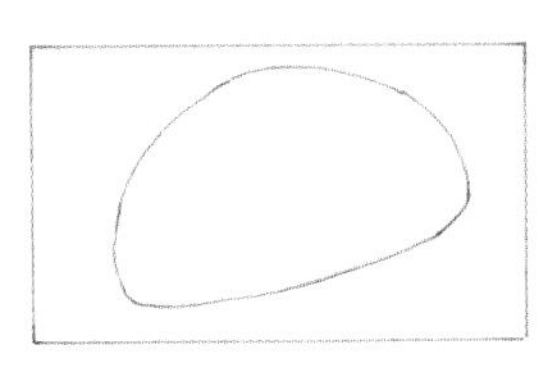

Fig 1

Fig 2

ADDING THE BORDER

3. Sew the text printed fabric strip to the left-hand side of the central panel (Fig 3). Sew the red spotted floral fabric strip to the top of the central panel, and the bright polka dot fabric strip to the bottom. Sew the grey floral fabric strip to the right-hand side. Press seams outwards.

Fig 3

QUILTING

4. Pin a piece of wadding (batting) behind the pillow front. Using white thread, quilt round the mushroom shape very close to the appliqué. Quilt round the central panel close to the borders and along the border edges. Using red embroidery cotton (floss), sew a decorative line of quilting stitches round the outside edge of the mushroom. Trim off excess wadding.

ASSEMBLING THE PILLOW

5. Take the backing fabric and trim it to the same size as the pillow front. Pin it right sides together with the pillow front. Sew all round, leaving a small gap for turning at the bottom (you could insert a zip here if you wish). Trim the seam, clip corners and turn right way out. Push the corners out and press the pillow.

6. Make a cushion pad (see Basic Techniques: Making a Cushion Pad). Insert the pad and slipstitch the gap closed. To finish, sew on the button in the left-hand corner of the central square, if you are using it.

Templates (full size)

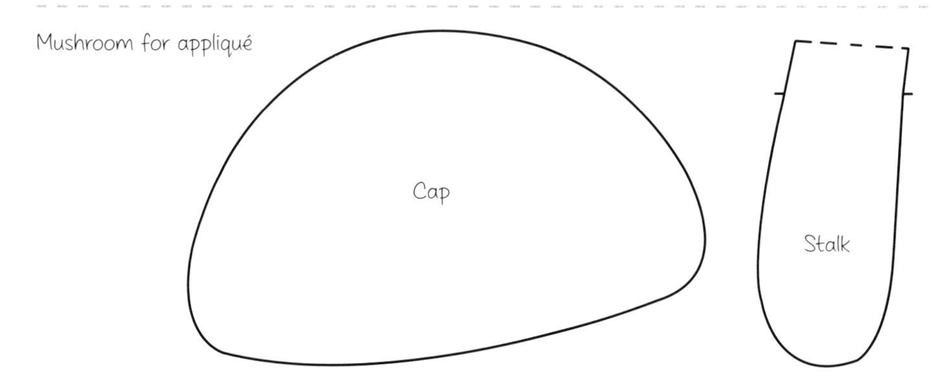

PUMPKIN PILLOW

This bright little autumn-inspired pillow looks lovely with the Mushroom Pillow, but works well alone, too. I love the warm, colourful shades of fabric used and how quick and easy it is to make. The use of fusible web for the appliqué means you can fix the shape neatly and quickly. The pumpkin motif could be used for other autumn-inspired makes, perhaps appliquéd to the front of a little felt Halloween bag for trick or treating, or as a repeating block for a little quilt.

You will need

- Yellow polka dot fabric for centre 6¾in (17cm) square
- Orange fabric for pumpkin 5in (12.5cm) square
- Green scraps of fabric for stem and leaves
- Bright polka dot fabric, two pieces for border each 3in x 10¼in (7.5cm x 26cm)
- Orange print fabric for border 2in x 6¾in (5cm x 17cm)
- White print fabric for border 2½in x 6¾in (6.5cm x 17cm)
- Green fabric for backing 11¾in x 7in for (30cm x 18cm)
- Cream fabric for backing 11¾in x 5½in (30cm x 14cm)
- Fusible web
- Lightweight wadding (batting) 6¼in (16cm) square
- Thin card for templates
- Orange and green embroidery cotton (floss)
- Big orange dotted button
- Cushion pad 9½in x 11in (24cm x 28cm)

FINISHED SIZE

9¾in x 11¼in (25cm x 28.5cm) approx.
Use ¼in (5mm) seam allowances

MAKING THE PUMPKIN

1. Take the orange and green fabrics and iron fusible web onto the backs. Trace the pumpkin template onto thin card and cut out. Do the same with the stem and leaf templates. Place the pumpkin card template on the back of the orange fabric and draw round the shape (Fig 1). Cut out carefully. Draw the stem and two leaves onto the back of the green fabric and cut out.

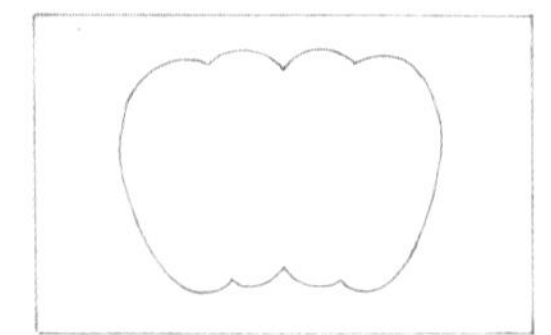
Fig 1

2. Place the pumpkin and stem on the yellow polka dot fabric with the bottom end of the stem just under the top edge of the pumpkin. Peel off the backing and iron the shapes in place. Position the leaves at the top of the stem and iron them in place (Fig 2).

Fig 2

3. Using one strand of orange embroidery cotton (floss) sew round the pumpkin with blanket stitch. Couch or backstitch three lines down the pumpkin to accentuate the shape. Using one strand of green and blanket stitch sew round the stem and leaves. Using one strand of green and backstitch sew the curling tendrils (see photo).

4. Place the wadding (batting) behind the appliqué and using white cotton thread quilt very closely round the pumpkin, stem and leaves. Quilt a square behind the pumpkin.

ADDING THE BORDER

5. Sew the white print fabric strip to the bottom of the central panel and the orange print strip to the top (Fig 3). Press seams outwards. Sew the bright polka dot fabric strips to the sides and press seams outwards. The patchwork should be 10¼in x 11¾in (26cm x 30cm), so trim if needs be.

Fig 3

MAKING UP THE PILLOW

6. To make the envelope-style back, take the green and cream fabric pieces and turn in one long edge on each piece, hem and press. Place the green fabric on top of the white fabric (both right side up), with the hemmed edges at the centre and aligning outer edges. Pin together along the hemmed edges. Place the pillow front on top, right side down, and pin together round the edges. Sew together all round. Trim the seams and clip the corners.

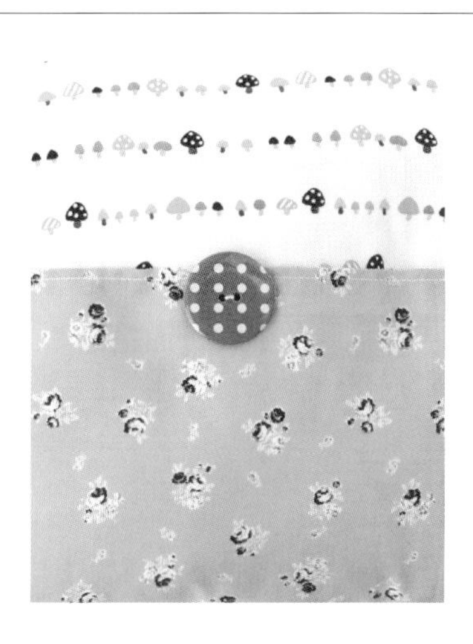

7. Remove the pins holding the envelope opening in place and turn the cover the right way out. Push out the corners and press. Make a cushion pad (see Basic Techniques: Making a Cushion Pad). Place the pad inside the cover and smooth neatly. Add a big button for decoration to the centre back if you wish.

Templates (full size)

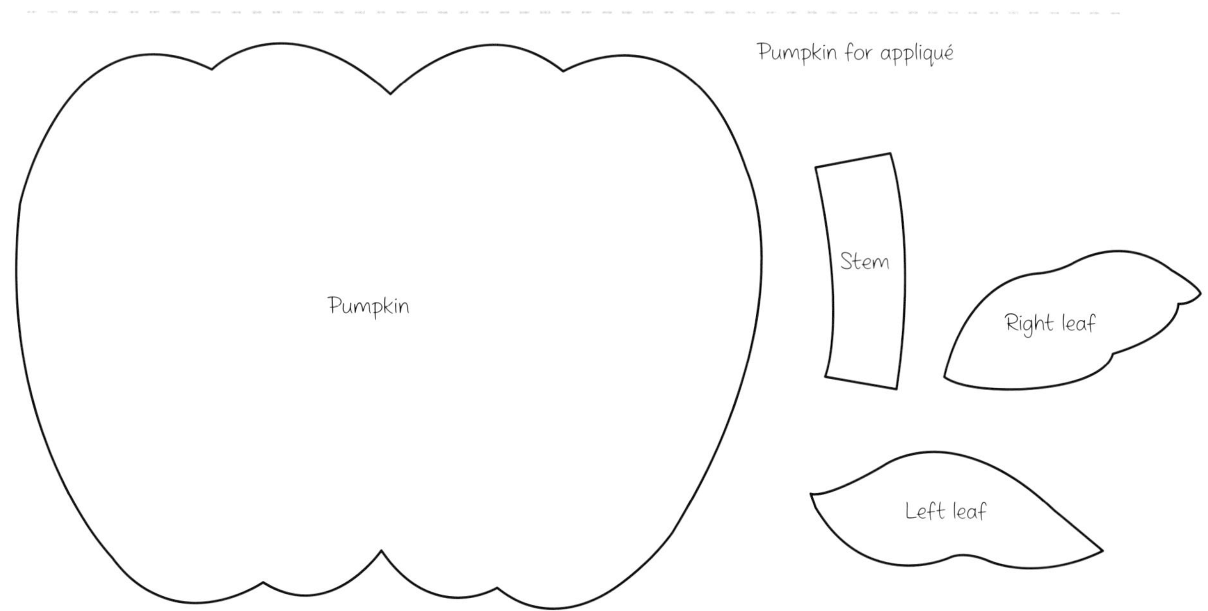

FABRIC PUMPKINS

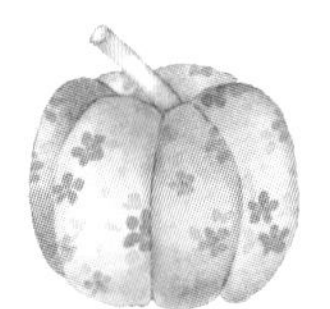

These fabric pumpkins are fun to make and look lovely clustered together to decorate the house in autumn. You can make them any size you like and in any sort of fabric you like. Mine are a modest size but you can make them very large or very tiny if you wish. The instructions are given for one pumpkin but the other pumpkins are made in exactly the same way.

You will need

- Print fabric for pumpkin 7in x 14in (18cm x 35.5cm)
- Sewing thread to suit fabric
- Polyester toy filling
- Green felt for stalk 1¾in x 2in (4.5cm x 5cm)
- Long needle
- Crochet cotton or yarn
- Hot glue gun or strong fabric glue

FINISHED SIZE

4in (10cm) approx. (largest pumpkin)
Use ¼in (5mm) seam allowances unless otherwise stated

SEWING THE PUMPKIN

1. Take the pumpkin fabric rectangle (Fig 1), fold it in half so right sides are facing and then sew a ¼in (5mm) seam down the side (Fig 2).

2. Using a sewing needle and matching thread, sew a running stitch along the bottom edge of the pumpkin (Fig 3). Pull up to gather the edge tightly and then fasten off.

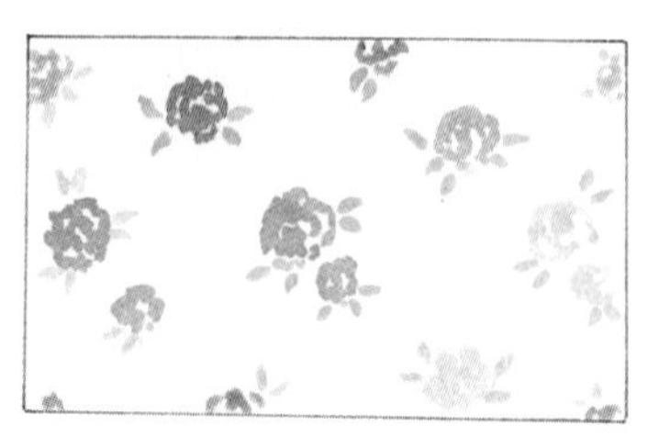

Fig 1

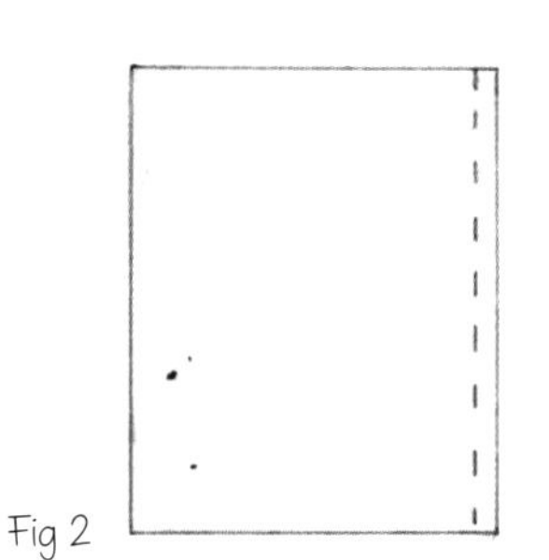

Fig 2

Fig 3

3. Turn the pumpkin out to the right side and stuff firmly, adding a lot of stuffing so it is very well filled. Sew another line of running stitch along the top of the pumpkin and pull it tight to gather as before (Fig 4). Fasten off securely.

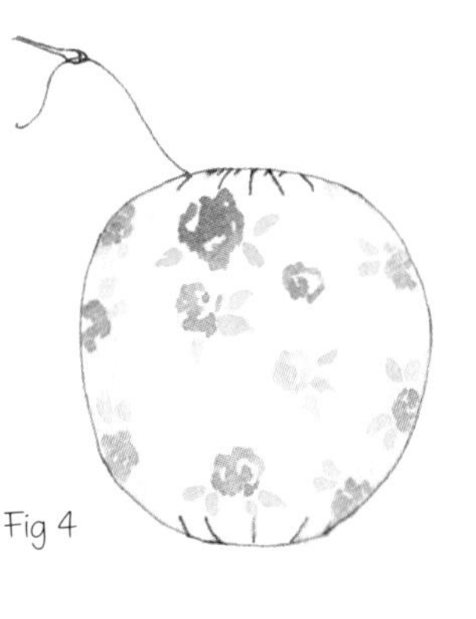

Fig 4

4. Take the long needle and about a 30in (75cm) length of crochet cotton. Beginning at the base of the pumpkin, push the needle right through the centre and back out at the top, then down and up again through the centre, forming a 'segment' each time (Fig 5). Make seven segments and then fasten off underneath the pumpkin.

Fig 5

5. To make the stalk, roll up the green felt and secure the edge of the roll with a little glue (Fig 6). Glue the stalk to the centre top of the pumpkin using a hot glue gun or strong glue.

Fig 6

tip

To make a larger or smaller pumpkin simply make the piece of fabric larger or smaller but keep the same proportions, that is, twice as wide as it is long.

CANDY DOLL QUILT

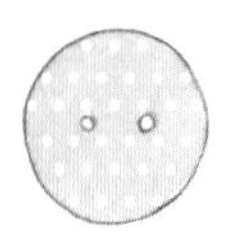

This gorgeous little doll's quilt is made using fresh, pretty colours and an English paper piecing technique, with the triangular patchwork pieces stitched together by hand. It is simple and fun to do and the results are very accurate. The square blocks are divided into four triangles and when placed next to each other and rotated they give a feeling of movement, which is perhaps why the original block was called the Big Dipper. The spotty buttons looked so pretty on their card near my completed quilt that I decided to add them. The goose cuddled up with the quilt in this little bed is a commercial toy but you could make the Bedtime Mouse instead.

You will need

- Assorted fabrics in fresh colours for triangles, scraps at least 2½in (6.5cm) square
- Solid white fabric for background triangles ¼yd (0.25m)
- Thin card for template
- Scrap paper for templates
- White sewing thread
- Novelty print backing fabric at least 15in x 12in (38cm x 30.5cm)
- Wadding (batting) at least 15in x 12in (38cm x 30.5cm)
- Binding fabric, fat quarter or ¼yd (0.25m)
- Twelve bright spotty buttons

FINISHED SIZE

15in x 12in (38cm x 30.5cm) approx.
Use ¼in (5mm) seam allowances

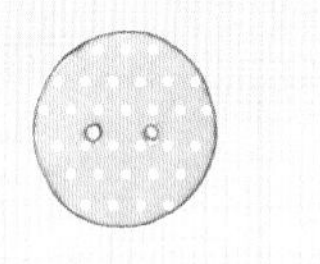

WORKING THE ENGLISH PAPER PIECING

1. Trace the triangle template onto thin card and cut out. Place the template onto scrap paper and draw round it carefully to make eighty paper triangles. For each square block you will need two white triangles and two matching patterned triangles. Using the template as a guide and adding a ¼in (5mm) seam allowance all round, cut out twenty pairs of patterned triangles and forty white triangles.

2. Take a paper triangle and pin it onto the wrong side of a fabric triangle (Fig 1). Fold the fabric triangle round it carefully, tacking (basting) in place. Repeat this with the remaining paper and fabric triangles.

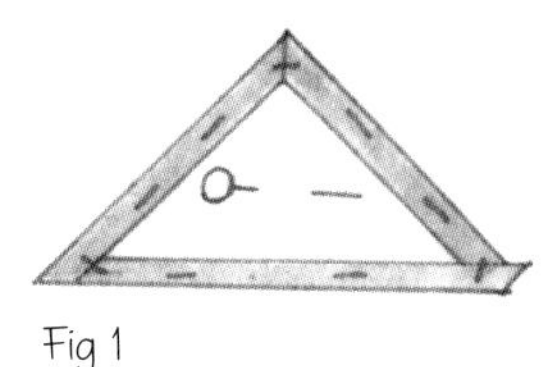

Fig 1

3. When you have covered all the paper triangles with fabric begin sewing the triangles together as shown in Fig 2, placing the pieces right sides together and whip stitching them neatly. Sew four triangles (two white and two patterned), into a square block. Continue in this way until you have sewn twenty blocks.

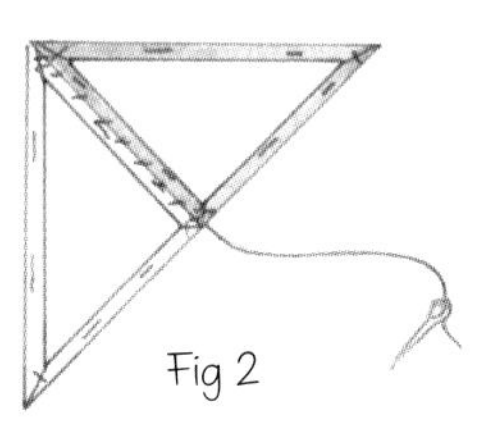

Fig 2

tip

If you prefer you could create templates by cutting 2in (5cm) squares of paper in half along one diagonal to make two triangles from each square.

ASSEMBLING THE QUILT

4. Lay out all the blocks, in four rows each with five blocks, rotating alternate blocks by 90 degrees, as shown in Fig 3 (see also the photo of the whole quilt). When you are happy with the layout, sew the blocks together by placing them right sides together and whip stitching the edges as before.

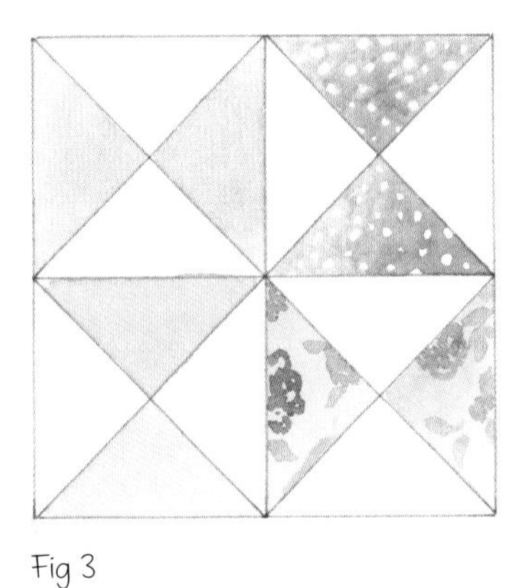

Fig 3

QUILTING AND FINISHING

5. Make a quilt sandwich by placing the backing fabric right side down on a table, the wadding (batting) on top and finally the patchwork top, right side up. Hold the layers in place using curved basting pins, tacking (basting) or other method of your choice.

6. Quilt round the triangles by hand, just inside the seam line, using white cotton.

7. Cut sufficient 2¼in (6.5cm) wide strips from the binding fabric to make a length of about 60in (150cm) when joined. Fold the binding in half along the length, wrong sides together and use this double-fold strip to bind the quilt, following the instructions in Basic Techniques: Binding. Finally, sew the spotty buttons to the corners of the central blocks as shown in the photograph.

Template (full size)

Triangle for English paper piecing

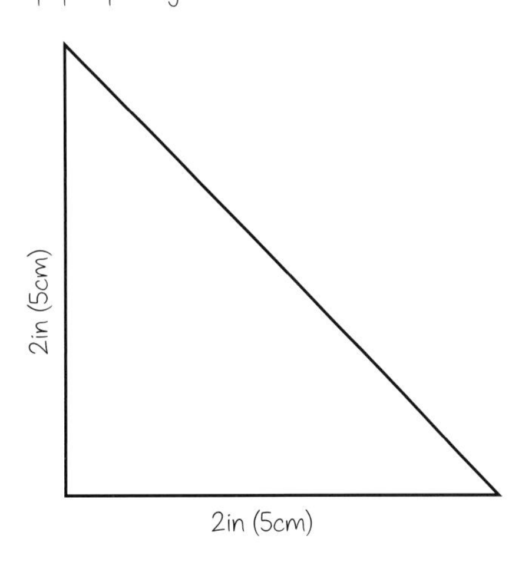

LITTLE BEAR

This little bear, made from soft cotton fabric and with wooden buttons used to create movable arms and legs, has a vintage style all of his own. He also has a patch or two sewn on to show he has been well loved, as he surely will be. He has a sweet bow around his neck with a little white painted bell. You could make this bear in any fabric you choose – bright and contemporary or soft and vintage – for many different kinds of bear all from the same pattern.

You will need

- Sand-coloured cotton fabric, about ¼yd (0.25m)
- Scraps of floral fabric for ears
- Fabric scraps for patches
- Thin card for templates
- Polyester toy filling
- Four wooden buttons
- Two black beads for eyes
- Black and red embroidery cotton (floss)
- Sewing threads to suit fabrics
- Fusible web
- Red gingham ribbon about 12in (30.5cm) long
- White bell
- Long needle and crochet cotton

FINISHED SIZE

9in (23cm) tall approx.
Use ¼in (5mm) seam allowances

tip

This bear is a decorative, collectable item and not suitable for children due to small parts, like the beads, button and bell. You could make it safe for children by omitting these and using embroidery instead.

CUTTING OUT

1. Trace the patterns onto thin card and cut out. Fold the sand-coloured fabric in half, lay the leg, arm and side body templates onto it and draw round the templates. Use only one fabric layer to draw the back of the body.

2 Place a piece of floral fabric right sides together with a piece of sand fabric and draw on the ear. Sew round the ears, cut out, turn right way out and press.

SEWING THE BEAR

3. Cut out the pieces for the body with a ¼in (5mm) seam allowance all round and pin the body pieces together as shown in Fig 1. Leave a gap in the seam for turning and gaps in the head for inserting the ears. Sew round the body. Turn the body the right way out and stuff firmly. Sew up the body gap neatly.

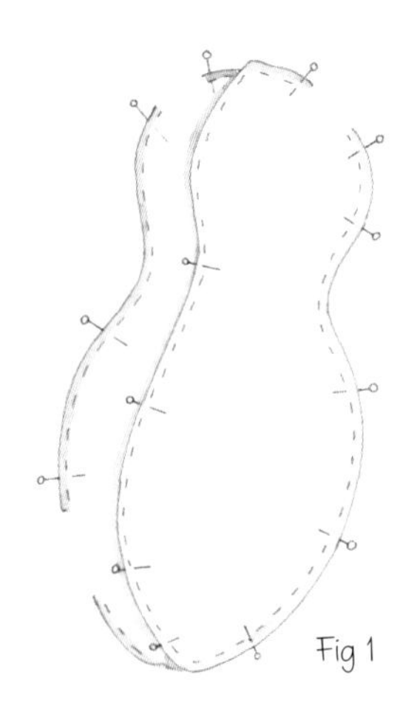

Fig 1

4. Insert the ears into the gaps left for them, pin and sew in place with matching thread (Fig 2).

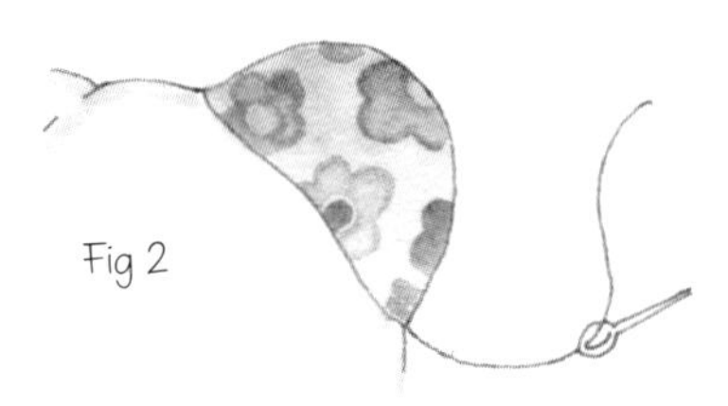

Fig 2

5. Sew round the arms and legs and then cut out and turn right side out. Press and then stuff firmly, sewing up the gaps.

6. To sew on the arms, thread a long needle with crochet cotton. Make a small stitch at the place where the first arm will go and then sew through the arm and through a wooden button. Come back through the arm and right through to the other side of the bear, through the second arm and the second wooden button (Fig 3). Sew back and forth until the arms feel secure and then fasten off. Attach the legs in the same way.

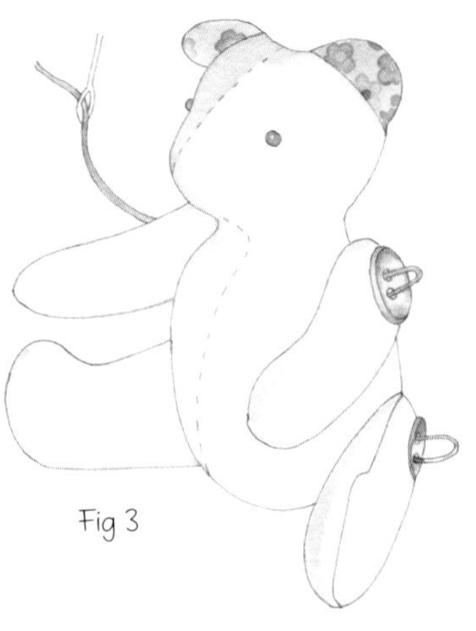

Fig 3

ADDING FEATURES AND EMBELLISHMENTS

7. Using black embroidery cotton (floss), satin stitch a nose and backstitch a mouth (see Basic Techniques: Stitches). Securely sew on two black beads for eyes (or use satin stitch). Add pink cheeks using blusher.

8. Iron fusible web on the back of two fabric scraps and fuse them to the front of the bear. Sew round them with red thread and big straight stitches. Put a bell onto red gingham ribbon and tie round the bear's neck.

Templates (full size)

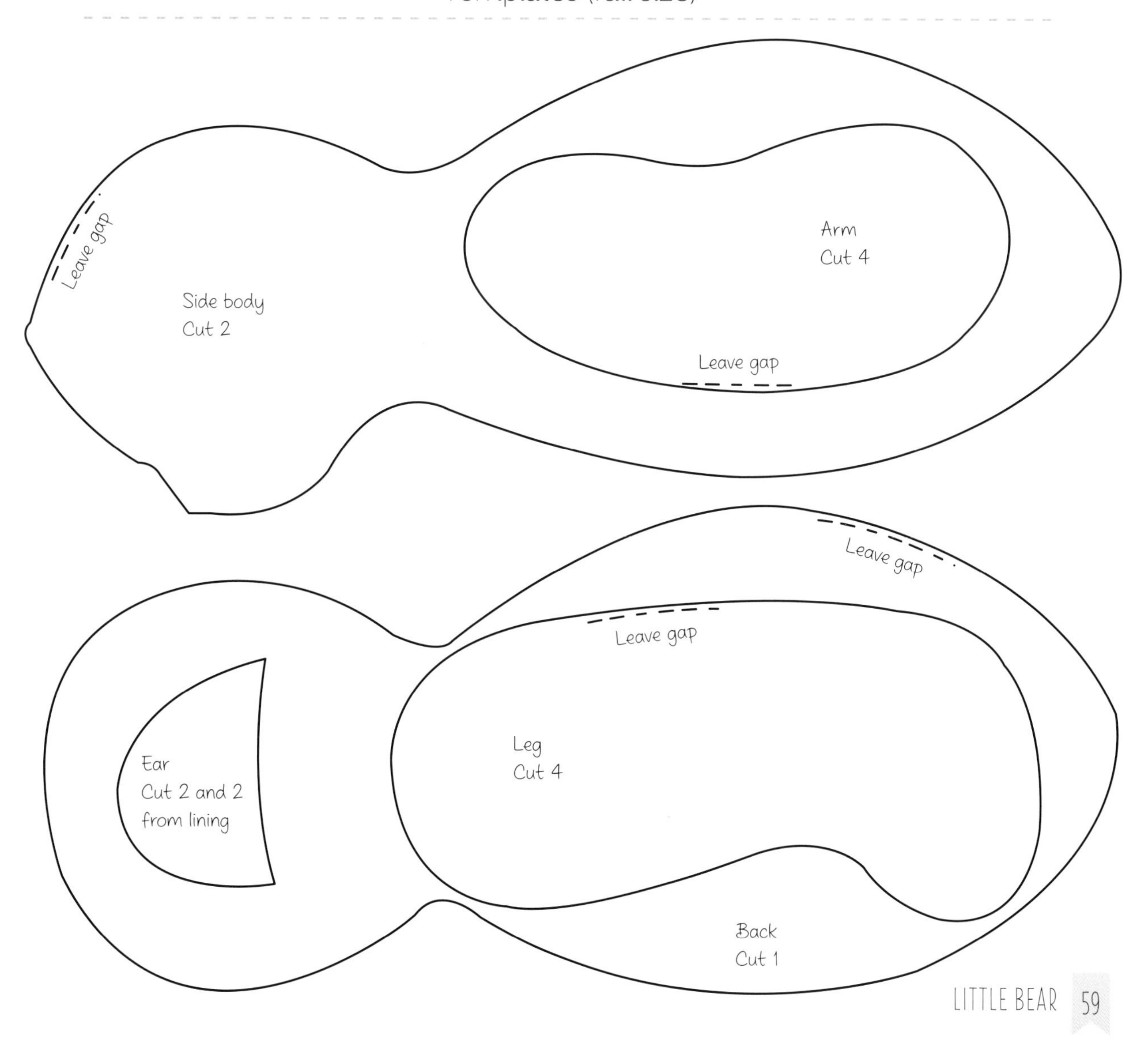

CHERRY POT HOLDER

I've always loved sewing hexagons, dating back to my schooldays when I first learnt how to do English paper piecing. I love the traditional Grandmother's Flower Garden blocks and how different they can look in new fabrics and used in new projects. This little pot holder also combines my love of cherries, which are so pretty and decorative and perfect for sewing on to kitchen items.

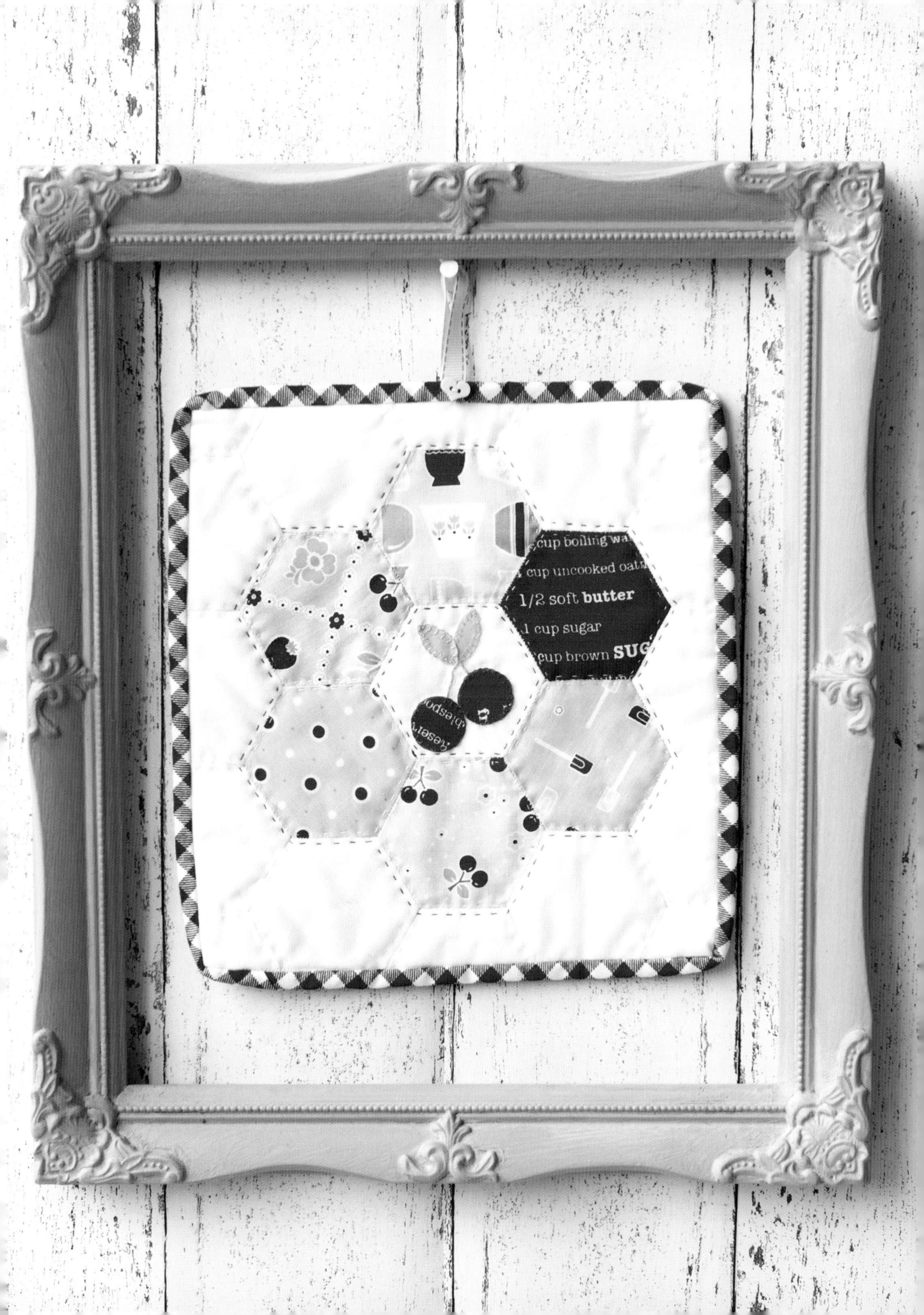

1/2 soft butter
cup sugar

You will need

- Scrap paper or seven 1¼in (3.2cm) hexagon paper pieces from purchased pack
- Six assorted fabric scraps in bright colours, each at least 3in (7.5cm) square
- White cotton fabric, fat quarter
- Thin card for template
- Fusible web
- Red and green embroidery cotton (floss)
- Wadding (batting) 9in (23cm) square
- Spotted pink and white backing fabric 9in (23cm) square
- Red gingham for binding ⅛yd (0.125m)
- Yellow ribbon for hanging loop 10in (25.5cm) long
- Tiny pink heart button (optional)

FINISHED SIZE

8½in x 8¼in (21.5cm x 21cm) approx.
Use ¼in (5mm) seam allowances unless otherwise stated

MAKING THE FABRIC HEXAGONS

1. Draw round the hexagon template on to thin card and cut out. Use the card template to draw seven hexagons on paper. Take a paper hexagon and cut a piece of coloured fabric ¼in (5mm) bigger all the way round. Pin the paper to the fabric shape (Fig 1). Fold the fabric round the hexagon and tack (baste) in place. Make five more hexagons in the same way. Make seventeen plain white ones for the centre and the rest of the block.

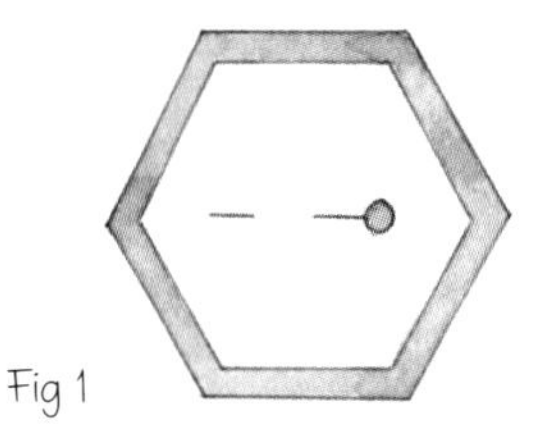
Fig 1

2. Lay out all of the hexagons as shown in the main photo and sew them together. Do this by placing two hexagons right sides together and whip stitching the edges together using white sewing thread (Fig 2). Add more hexagons to complete the layout.

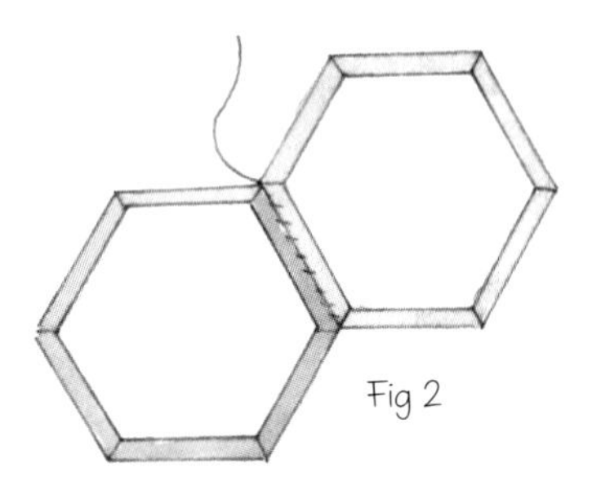
Fig 2

ADDING THE APPLIQUÉ

3. Take a small scrap of red fabric and another of green fabric and iron fusible web onto the wrong side. Trace two cherries and two leaves from the templates and copy onto the paper side of the fusible web. Cut them out carefully.

4. Remove the paper shape from the back of the centre white hexagon. Position the cherries and leaves in the centre. When happy with the position, peel off the web paper and iron in place (Fig 3). Use red embroidery cotton (floss) and blanket stitch to sew round the cherries. Use green and blanket stitch to sew round the leaves. Use backstitch and green to stitch two stems.

5. Remove all the paper pieces from the rest of the block. Fold in the edges until the block measures 8½in x 8¼in (21.5cm x 21cm). Press and trim excess.

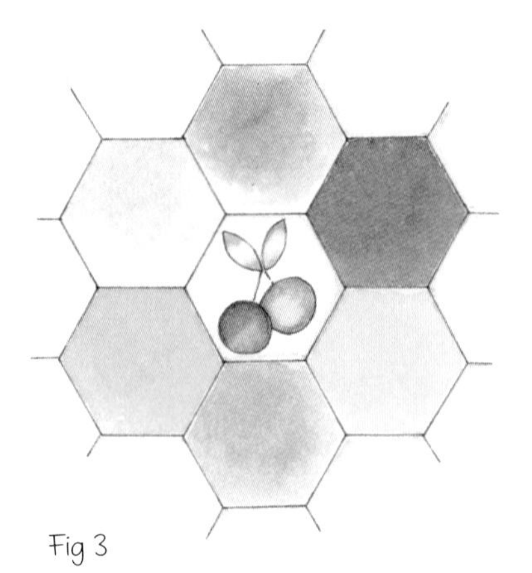
Fig 3

QUILTING AND FINISHING

6. Place the backing fabric right side down, put the wadding (batting) on top and the patchwork block on top, right side up. Pin or tack (baste) the layers in place. Using red embroidery cotton (floss), quilt round the inner white hexagon and the outer hexagon shapes (Fig 4). Using white sewing thread, quilt all the white hexagons and round the cherries and leaves. Trim the backing and wadding level with the quilted front.

7. Cut sufficient 2¼in (6cm) wide strips from the red gingham binding fabric to make a length

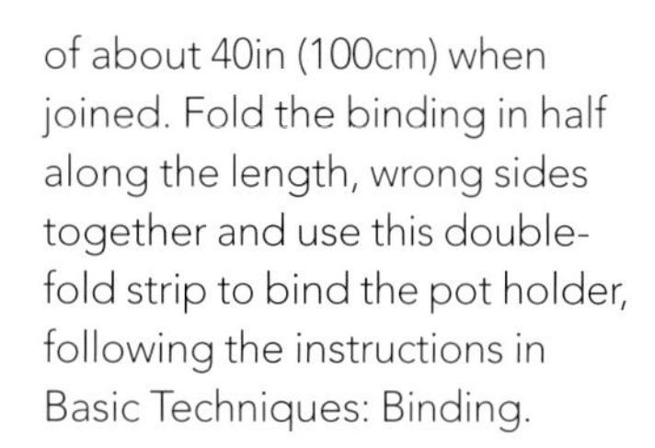

of about 40in (100cm) when joined. Fold the binding in half along the length, wrong sides together and use this double-fold strip to bind the pot holder, following the instructions in Basic Techniques: Binding.

8. To finish, fold the yellow ribbon in half and sew to the top of the pot holder, at the back. Sew on a small pink heart button at the top front.

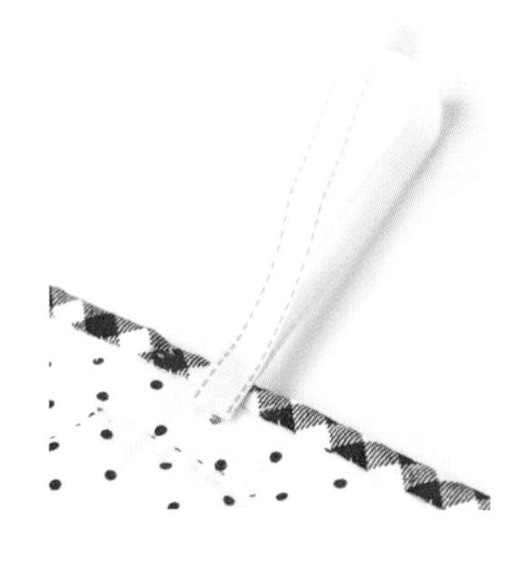

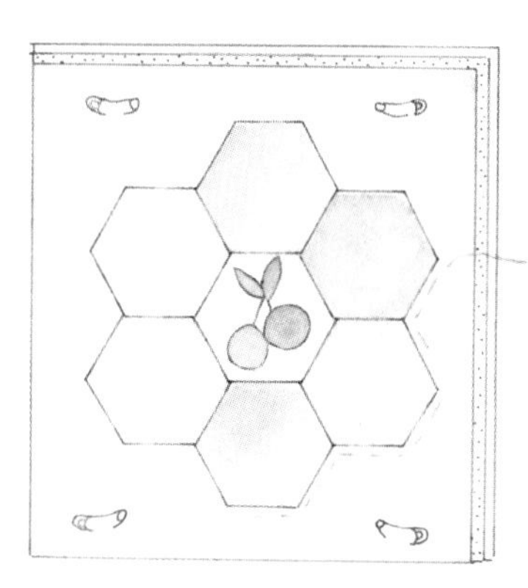

Fig 4

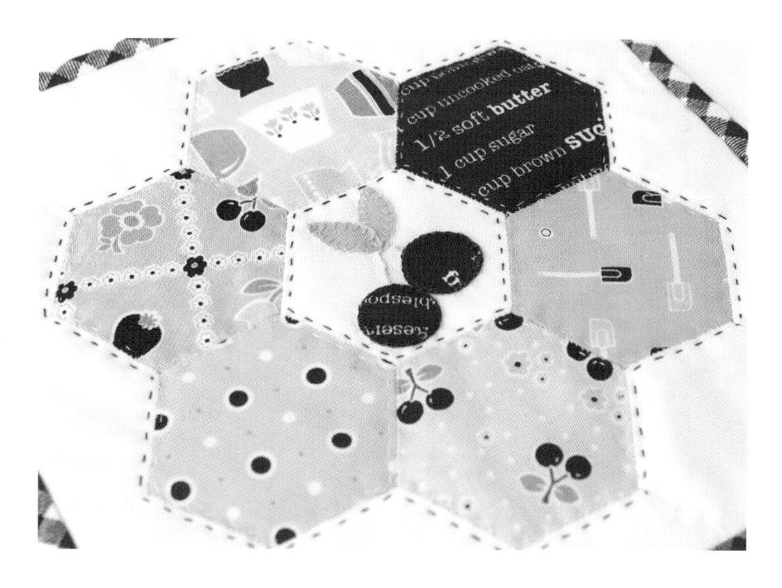

Templates (full size)

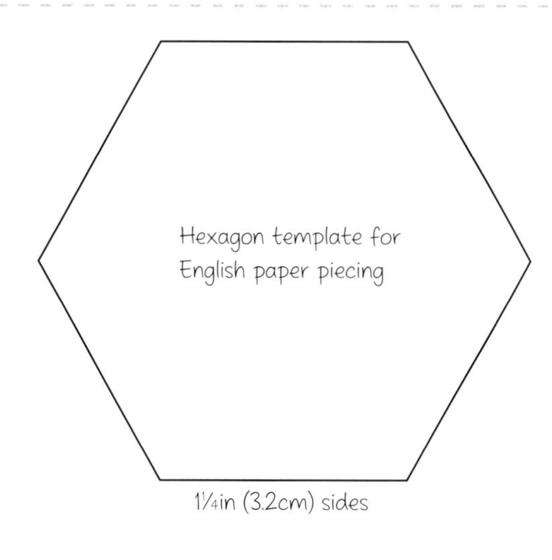

1¼in (3.2cm) sides

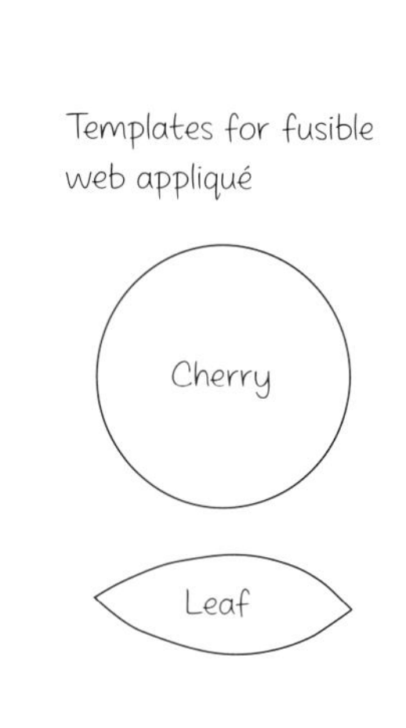

Bedtime Mouse

This darling little mouse, with her pretty nightdress, pillow and patchwork quilt, would make a lovely gift for a small girl – or even for a bigger girl! The postage stamp quilt is so tiny, just right for a mouse, and the little pillow completes this adorable set. It's the perfect project for using up little scraps of sweet fabrics.

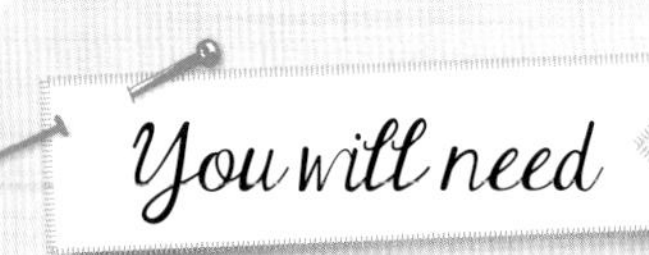

For the mouse and nightdress

- Pale pink cotton fabric, fat quarter
- Scraps of pink/white gingham
- Orange bead for nose
- Sewing threads to suit fabrics
- Black embroidery cotton (floss)
- Thin card for templates
- Blusher (optional)
- Polyester toy filling
- Two pieces of pale blue floral fabric 7in x 6in (18cm x 15cm)
- Shirring elastic

For the quilt and pillow

- Scraps of cotton fabrics, thirty 1½in (3.5cm) squares
- Backing fabric 5½in x 6½in (14cm x 16.5cm)
- Blue floral fabric, two pieces 2½in x 3½in (6.3cm x 9cm)
- Tiny buttons (optional)
- Polyester toy filling

FINISHED SIZE

Mouse: 7in x 6in (18cm x 15cm) approx
Quilt: 5in x 6in (12.5cm x 15.2cm)
Pillow: 3in x 2in (7.5cm x 5cm)
Use ¼in (5mm) seams unless otherwise stated

MAKING THE MOUSE AND NIGHTDRESS

1. Use the templates to trace the body, arms and legs onto thin card and cut out. Fold the pink cotton in half (right sides together if using a print) and trace the templates onto it. Don't cut out until sewing is complete.

2. Following the drawn lines, sew around the body, arms and legs, backstitching, by machine or hand (Fig 1).

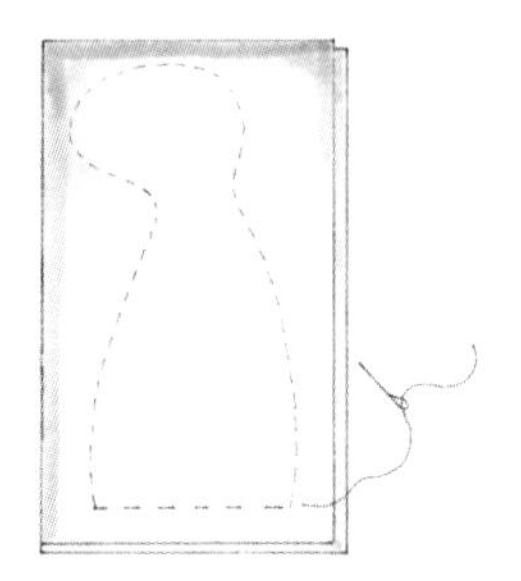

Fig 1

3. Cut out two ears from pink cotton and two ear linings from gingham. Place the pieces right sides together and sew round the curve. Turn out and press.

4. Cut out the pieces ¼in (5mm) from the sewn lines, turn right side out and press. Stuff the body with filling, with the seam at front middle. Stuff the legs and place the tops inside the body with the feet facing front. Sew across the bottom body seam, catching the legs in the seam (Fig 2). Stuff the arms and sew to either side of the body.

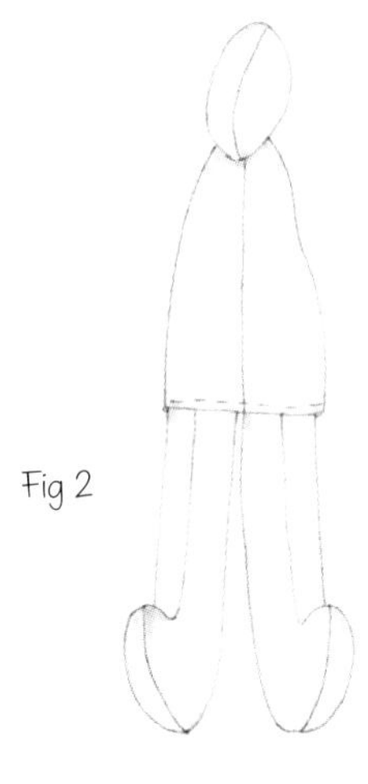

Fig 2

5. Sew along the bottom of the ears and gather up. Sew an ear to each side of the head (Fig 3).

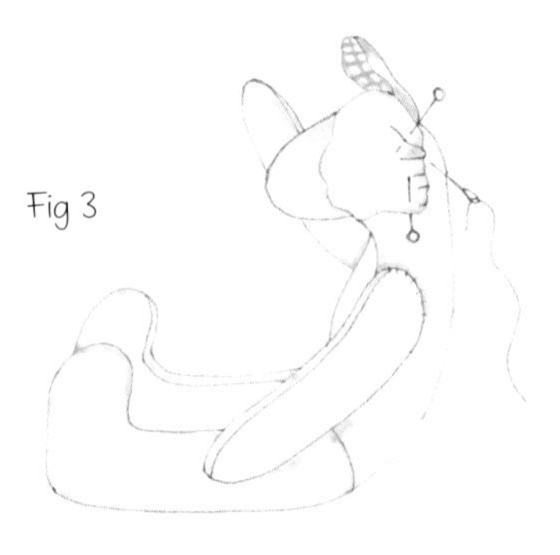

Fig 3

6. Make the face by sewing eyes with two strands of black embroidery cotton (floss) and French knots. Sew a mouth with black backstitch. Sew on an orange bead nose. If the toy is for a baby you could sew the nose with orange satin stitch instead.

7. Trace the nightdress template onto thin card and cut out. Fold the blue floral fabric in half, right sides together, and place the pattern on the fold line. Cut out two pieces for the back and front.

8. Sew up the side seams, join the shoulders. Turn a small hem along the bottom. Turn a tiny hem in at the neck and cuffs, and sew along with running stitch and shirring elastic. Pull up the elastic to gather the cuffs and neck to fit the mouse and tie off.

MAKING THE QUILT AND PILLOW

9. Take the thirty 1½in (3.5cm) squares and arrange in a 6 x 5 layout. Sew together in rows (Fig 4). Sew the rows together by hand or machine. Press the patchwork carefully.

10. Place the backing fabric right sides together with the patchwork. Sew all around, leaving a gap at one side for turning through. Turn right side out and push out the corners. Sew up the gap and press. Using white sewing thread, topstitch close to the edge all round (Fig 4). If you wish, add some embellishments, such as tiny buttons and an appliqué heart.

Fig 4

11. For the pillow, put the two pieces of blue floral fabric right sides together. Sew round the edges, leaving a small gap. Turn through to the right side, push out the corners and press. Stuff lightly with toy filling and sew the gap closed.

tip

You don't have to buy a bed for the mouse to sleep in – it's easy to make one by covering a small box with pretty paper.

Templates (full size)

Dashed lines show where one part fits into another

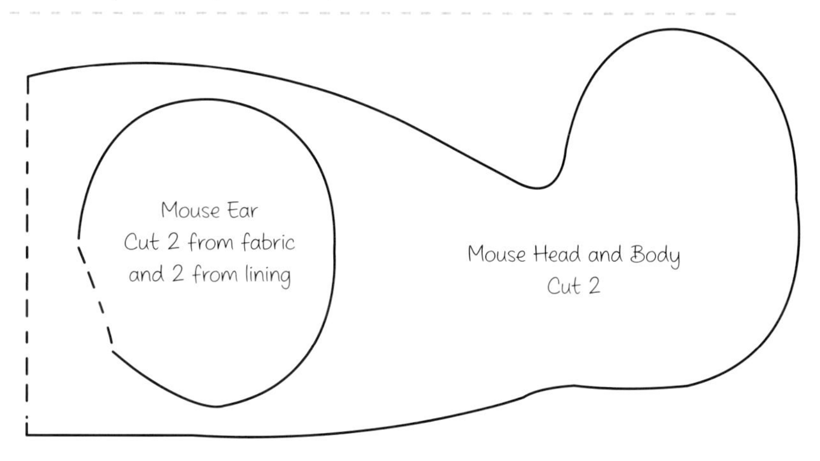

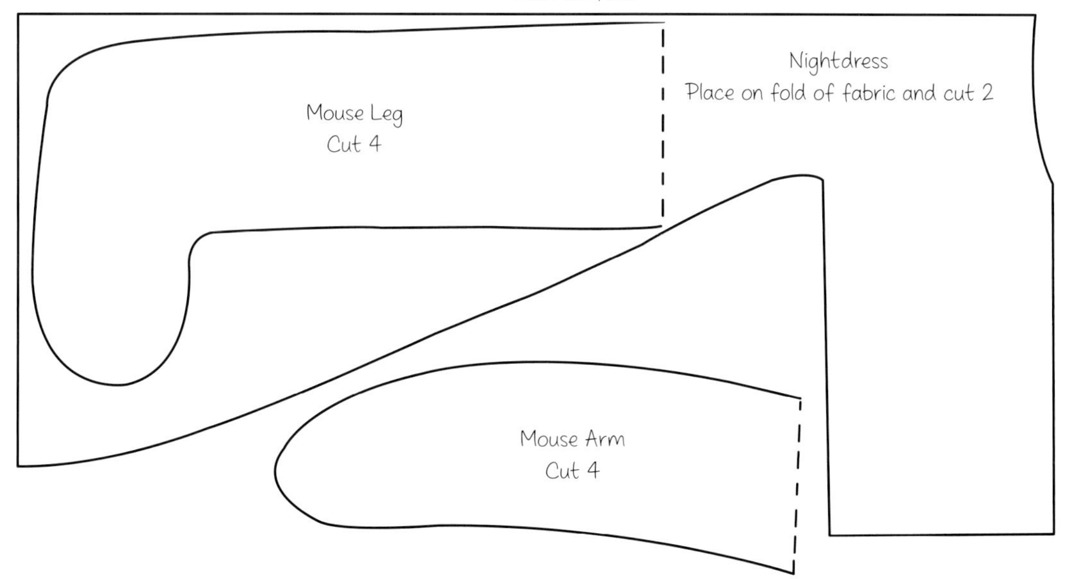

CHRISTMAS ANGEL

This Christmas angel is a very special kind of doll, one that you may like to keep for many festive seasons. You can make her as pretty and as magical as you wish. This little angel has beautiful wings, a dress trimmed with cotton lace and a little bit of net petticoat peeping out, as well as a tiny, rustic halo. You can have fun raiding your stash for embellishments to make your very own Christmas angel.

listen
turn left
Tulips,
in a row.
a baby

You will need

- Thin card for templates
- Pink cotton fabric for doll body ½yd (0.5m)
- Polyester toy filling
- Light beige wool yarn for hair
- Tissue paper
- Double-sided adhesive tape
- Cream floral fabric for dress ¼yd (0.25m)
- Cream cotton lace
- Pink net 2in x 13in (5cm x 33cm)
- Text print fabric for wings 16in (40.5cm) square
- Red and white sewing thread
- Florist's wire, silver-grey raffia and tiny cream ribbon roses for halo
- Fine fabric marker in black and blusher for features
- Strong fabric glue or glue gun

FINISHED SIZE

13in (35cm) tall approx.
Use ¼in (5mm) seam allowances unless otherwise stated

MAKING THE ANGEL

1. The angel uses the same body patterns and instructions as the Sweet Doll project. Fold the pink fabric in half and lay all the templates except the wings on top. Follow steps 1–6 of the Sweet Doll to make the doll and the hair.

2. For the halo take an 8in (20cm) length of red florist's wire, measure it round the angel's head and then wind the ends together so it fits snugly but not too tightly. Wind a strand of silver-grey raffia round the wire frame. Secure with a dab of glue. Attach four (or more) small ribbon roses to the halo with strong glue or a glue gun.

3. For the wings, copy the wings template onto thin card. Place two pieces of text print fabric right sides together and draw round the wings template on one side (Fig 1). Sew round the shape leaving a small gap on one side for turning. Trim the seams and turn right side out, carefully pushing out the points. Press, sew the gap closed and then stitch a line of running stitch round the edge of the wings using red sewing thread.

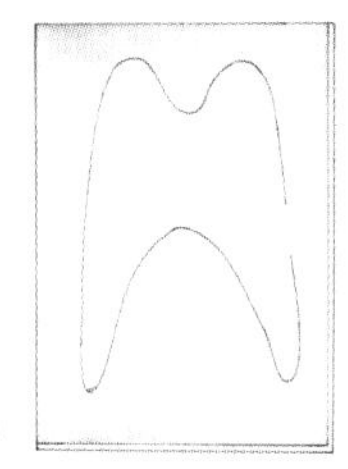

Fig 1

MAKING THE DRESS

4. Trace the bodice templates onto thin card and cut out. Take the floral fabric, draw round the bodice shapes onto the back and cut them out.

5. Sew round the sleeves with a small hem and then sew up the side seams and shoulders. Cut a piece of the same fabric for the skirt 7in x 13in (18cm x 35cm). Sew a small hem at the bottom edge and sew a length of cream cotton lace along it. Attach a strip of pink net to the inside of the hem so it shows just below the edge of the lace.

6. Gather the skirt until it fits the bodice. Pin and tack (baste) in place and then machine sew the dress together along the seam. Sew up the back seam. Sew a piece of cotton lace round the

waist (Fig 2). Gather a length of the same lace to make a ruffle for the neck. Put the dress on the angel, gather the neck and sew on the lace ruffle. Sew the back bodice seam closed.

7. Attach the wings to the centre of the back using strong fabric glue or a hot glue gun (Fig 3). To finish, add the halo to the head, at a slight angle.

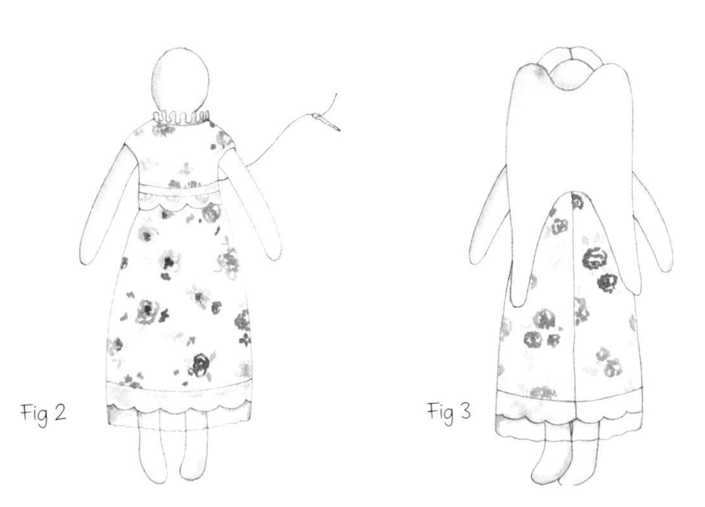
Fig 2 Fig 3

Templates (full size)

For the angel body use the templates from the Sweet Doll chapter

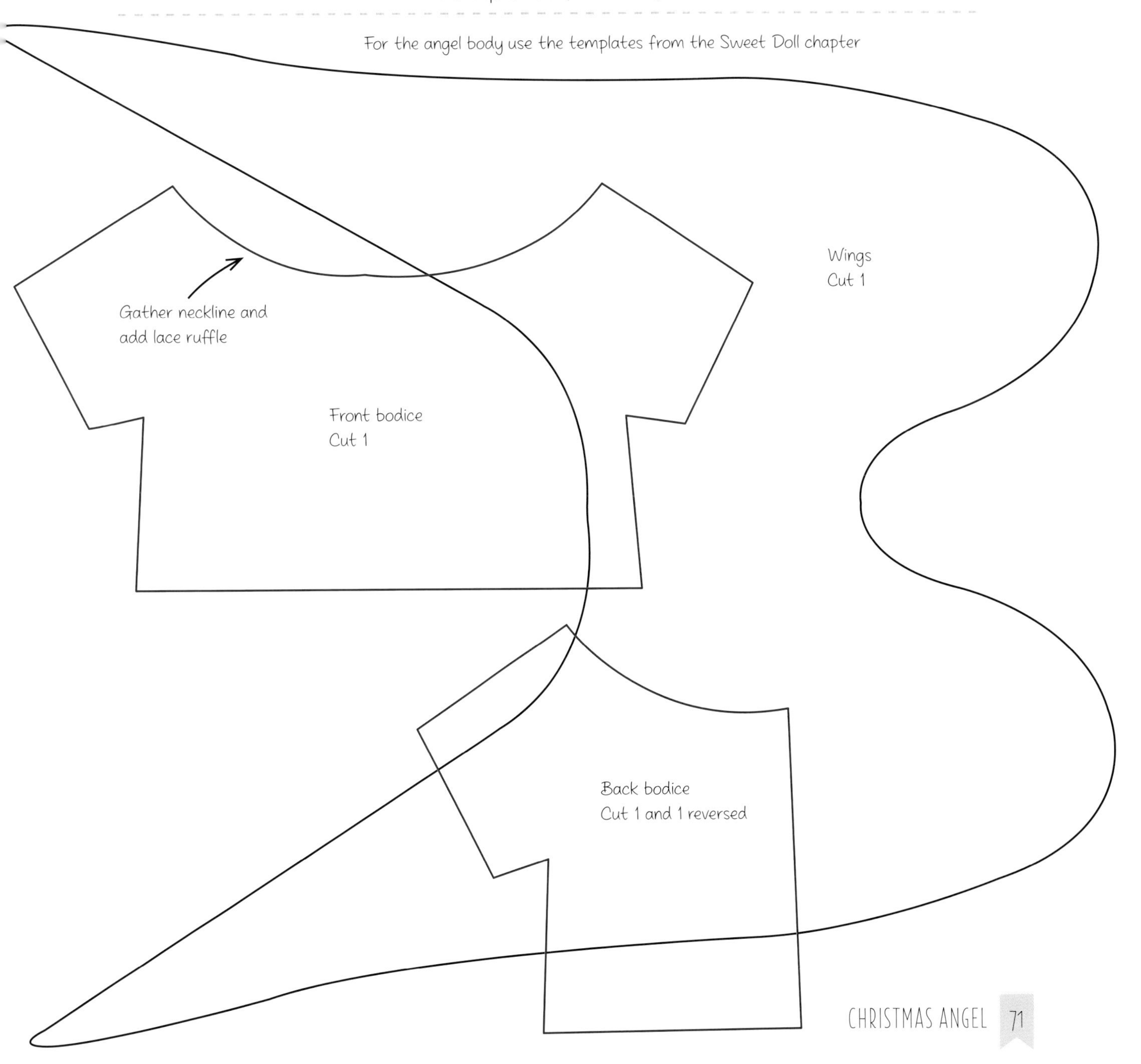

BIG FLOWER PILLOW

This pretty flower pillow would make a lovely gift for a girl of any age. It uses colourful scrap fabrics to create the appliqué flower petals and can be made in any colour scheme, for an individual look or to suit a special room. The flower is easy to create using a template and fusible web appliqué. The cushion cover is made in an envelope style, with added binding round the edge to make it extra special.

You will need

- Pale pink fabric for front 14½in (40cm) square
- Pink spotty backing fabric two pieces each 10in x 14½in (25.5cm x 40cm)
- Eight assorted pink and blue fabrics for petals, each about 2in x 5in (5cm x 12.5cm)
- Two different green fabric scraps for centre
- Scrap of red print for covering button
- Fusible wadding (batting) 14½in (40cm) square
- Fusible web
- Thin card
- Very pale grey and green sewing thread
- Masking tape (optional)
- One self-cover button
- Cushion pad 14in (35.5cm) square

XXXXXXXXXXXXXXXXXXXXXX

FINISHED SIZE

14½in (40cm) square approx. Use ¼in (5mm) seam allowances unless otherwise stated

CREATING THE FLOWER

1. Trace the petal and centre circle onto thin card and cut out to make the templates. Iron fusible web onto the back of the blue and pink petal fabrics and one scrap of green fabric. Draw round the petal template onto the back of the fabrics to create eight petals and cut out carefully. Draw round the circle template onto the back of the green fabric and cut out.

2. Take the pressed pale pink fabric square and put the petals in place on it. Peel off the backing paper and iron the petals in place (Fig 1).

Fig 1

3. Sew round each petal using pale grey sewing cotton and blanket stitch. Take the green centre circle and iron it in place in the middle of the flower, and then sew round it with green sewing thread and blanket stitch.

QUILTING

4. Take the lightweight fusible wadding (batting) and place it behind the pillow front, securing with pins or curved safety pins here and there. Using very pale grey sewing thread, quilt round the petal shapes (Fig 2). Quilt some straight lines in the background using masking tape to mark a straight guideline if required (Fig 3). You can quilt as much or as little as you wish.

Fig 2

Fig 3

MAKING UP

5. For the backing, take the two pieces of pink spotty fabric and turn a ½in (1.5cm) hem on one long side of each. These will form the centre edge of the opening across the back of the cushion. Press the hems, then overlap them and pin together on the right side, across the long central edges (Fig 4). Place the back and the front of the pillow wrong sides together and sew round the four sides. Trim the seams and clip the corners.

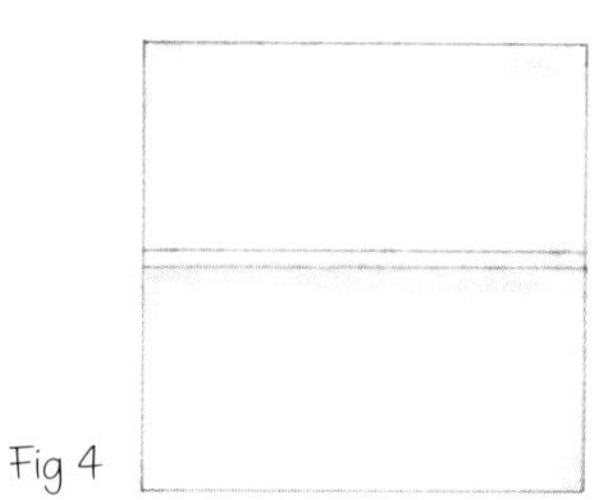

Fig 4

6. Cut sufficient 2½in (6.5cm) wide strips from the binding fabric to make a length of about 65in (165cm) when joined. Press the seams open. Fold the binding in half along the length, wrong sides together and use this double-fold strip to bind the edge of the cushion, following the instructions in Basic Techniques: Binding.

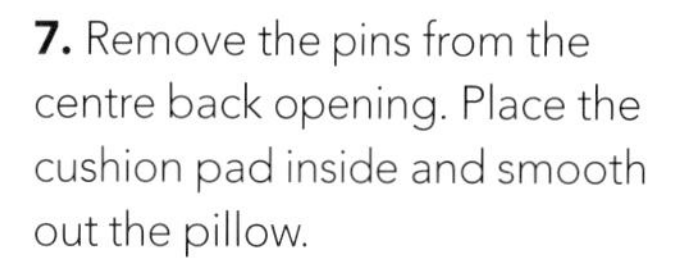

7. Remove the pins from the centre back opening. Place the cushion pad inside and smooth out the pillow.

MAKING A YO-YO

8. Cut a 3¼in (8cm) diameter circle from the remaining green fabric scrap. Sew a line of running stitch just inside the circle, pull up to gather and fasten off. Neaten the folds of the yo-yo and then sew it to the flower centre. Finish off by covering the button with red print fabric (following the manufacturer's instructions) and then sew the button to the centre of the yo-yo.

Templates (full size)

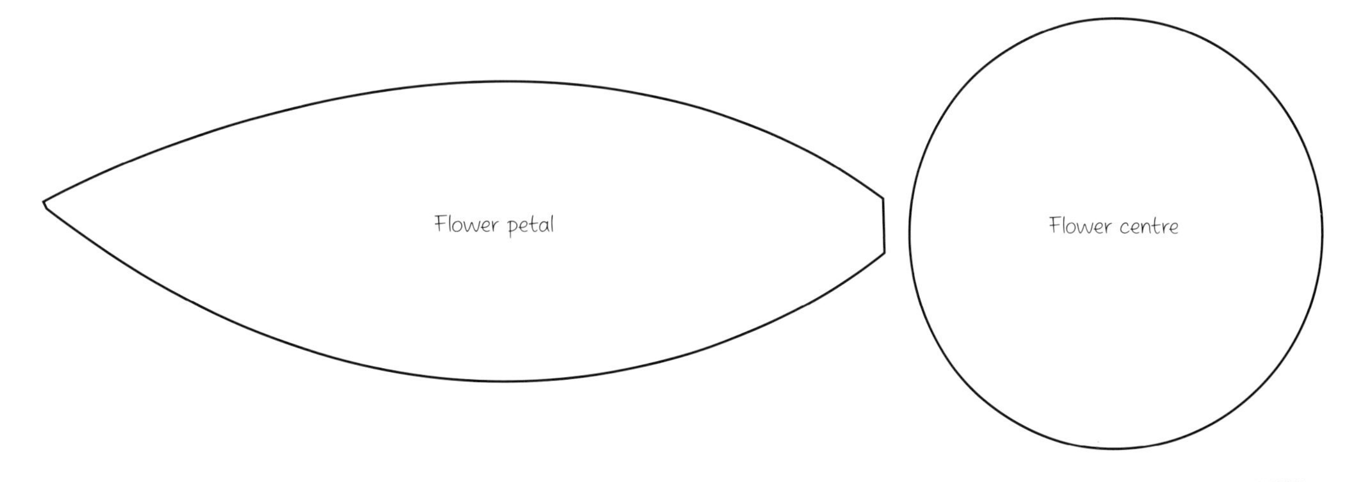

RAINBOW BIRDS

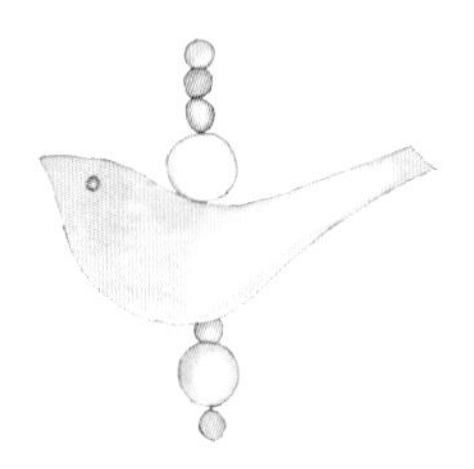

Small stitched fabric birds have been made throughout history and are a popular project for present-day crafters. The birds can be made as an individual decoration, or you can make several and string them together as I have here. This garland of rainbow birds is simple and fun to make, using an assortment of solid colour fabrics. You could also raid your scrap bin and make the birds in a host of colourful printed fabrics, too.

You will need

- Solid cotton fabrics in pink, red, yellow, green, blue, purple and aqua – each bird needs two pieces of fabric about 4in x 5½in (10cm x 14cm)
- Thin card for template
- Polyester toy filling
- Black sewing thread
- Beading needle
- Dark grey petite seed beads for eyes
- Assortment of colourful beads of varying sizes
- Pink/white baker's twine
- Large-eyed needle

FINISHED SIZE

20in (50cm) long approx. Use ¼in (5mm) seam allowances unless otherwise stated

MAKING THE BIRDS

1. Trace the bird template onto a piece of thin card and cut out carefully. Take two pieces of fabric each 4in x 5½in (10cm x 14cm) and trace the bird template onto the top piece, leaving a small gap as on the template. Sew round the bird shape, leaving a gap where marked for turning out (Fig 1).

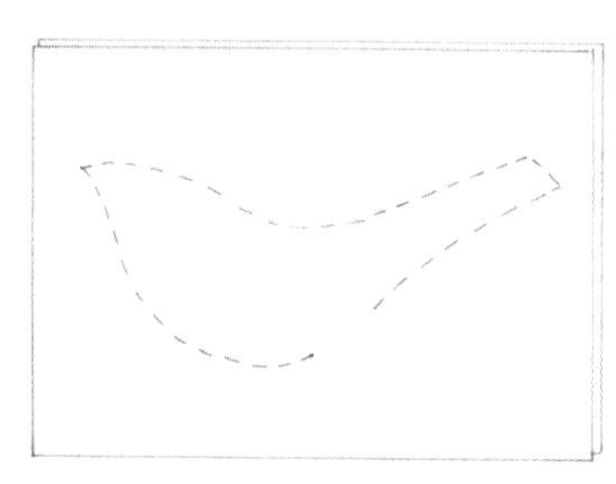

Fig 1

2. Cut out the bird leaving a ¼in (5mm) allowance all round and turn right side out. Make sure the tail and beak are pushed out, and then fill with polyester toy filling. Sew up the gap neatly (Fig 2).

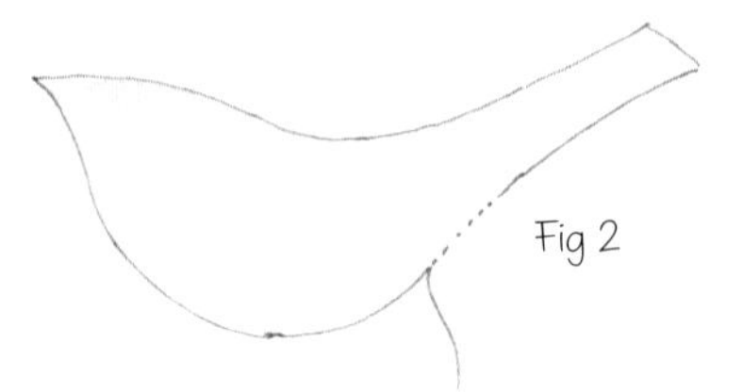

Fig 2

3. Using black sewing thread and a beading needle sew on two petite seed beads to either side of the bird's head for eyes.

4. Using the same process, make six more birds from the different fabric colours.

ASSEMBLING THE HANGING

5. Thread a large-eyed needle with a long piece of twine and tie a big knot at the end. Thread on a few colourful beads. Starting at the bottom of the first bird, push the needle right through the bird from bottom to top (Fig 3). Add another set of beads and then sew through another bird. Continue until all the birds have been added.

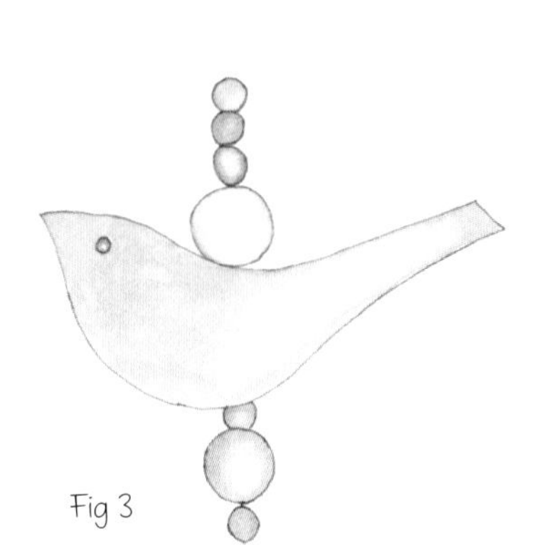

Fig 3

6. String extra beads at the top to finish off the hanging. Tie a secure knot and then tie the remaining baker's twine into a loop for hanging.

Template (full size)

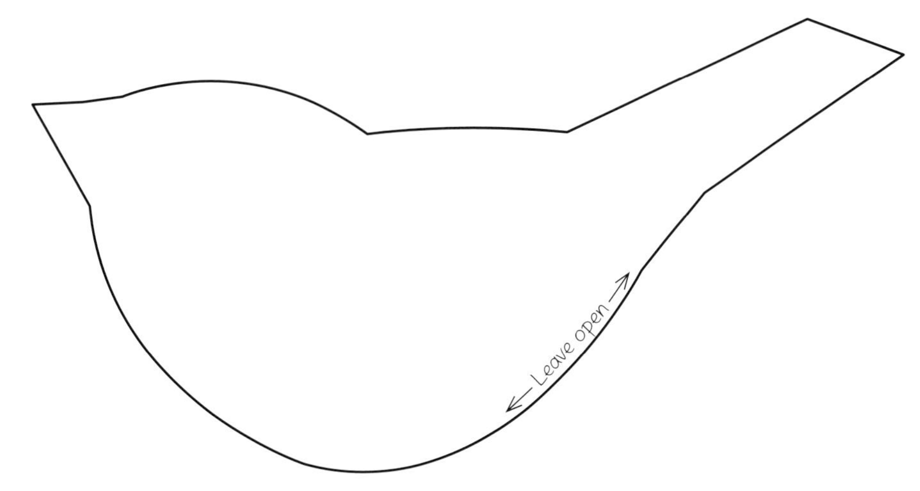

SPRING BIRD HEARTS

I love to make hearts for all kinds of reasons – to hang in my home, to give as gifts on different occasions, to use up scraps of favourite fabrics, and because they are endlessly fun to embellish. These contemporary hearts were made to celebrate the start of spring, with soft pretty colours and little birds and flower buttons to evoke the season. You could add word greetings, too, if you wished.

DARLINGTON
POST CARD
DARLINGTON

You will need

For three hearts

- Striped and floral fabrics, about 4in x 7in (10cm x 18cm) for each heart
- Scraps of blue or mauve fabric for appliqué birds
- Thin card for template
- Polyester toy filling
- Fusible web
- White sewing thread
- Garden twine
- Raffia
- Three flower buttons
- Erasable pen

FINISHED SIZE

3½in x 3¾in (9cm x 9.5cm) each heart approx.
Use ¼in (5mm) seam allowances unless otherwise stated

MAKING A HEART

1. Trace the heart template onto thin card and cut out. Fold a piece of striped heart fabric in half, place the heart template in the centre and draw round the template using an erasable pen (Fig 1). Sew round the heart carefully, by hand or machine, following the marked line.

2. Cut a small opening in the back for turning through. Turn the heart the right way out, push out the edges and press. Stuff the heart firmly with polyester toy filling and sew up the opening in the back (Fig 2).

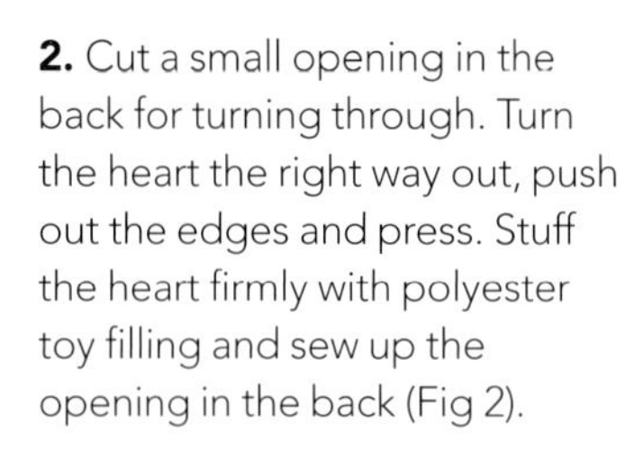

Fig 1

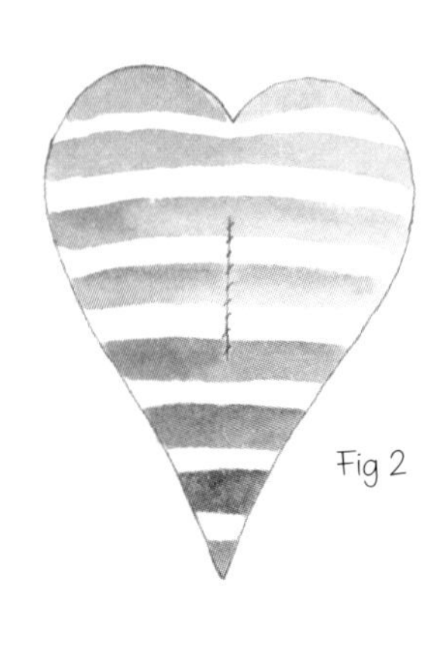

Fig 2

ADDING THE APPLIQUÉ

3. Take a piece of blue or mauve fabric and iron fusible web on the back. Trace the bird motif onto it and cut out. Place the bird on the front of the heart, peel off the backing and iron the bird in place.

4. Sew all round the bird using running stitch and white sewing thread. Sew an extra row of running stitch round the outside of the bird to echo the shape. Sew on a flower button above the bird (Fig 3).

Fig 3

5. Following the same process, make two more hearts, one striped and one floral.

FINISHING OFF

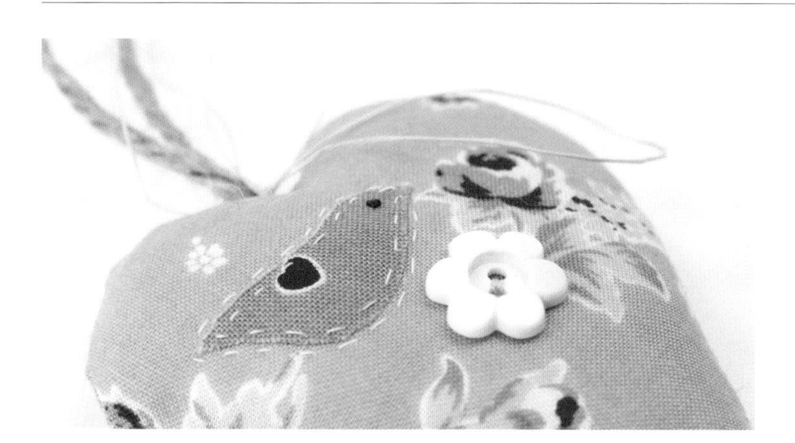

6. Take a piece of twine about 8in (20cm) long, fold it in half and then sew it to the top of a heart. Tie a thin piece of raffia into a bow round the twine. Repeat for the other two hearts to finish.

Templates (full size)

tip

You could use this idea to make other hearts, varying the fabrics for the occasion. For example, you could look for pretty, Easter-themed fabrics and decorative buttons with bunnies, carrots and eggs.

HEXAGON DRAWSTRING BAG

This little bag is very pretty and can be used to store all kinds of things, from sewing and craft items to jewellery. It would make a lovely gift in itself too, especially if it contained a small treat. The hexagon patchwork is easily made using the English paper piecing method and is a great way to use up favourite scraps of pretty fabric.

You will need

- Thin card for master template
- Scrap paper for templates
- Scraps of assorted floral fabrics, each about 3in (7.5cm) square
- Coordinating fabric 11½in x 2¼in (30cm x 6cm)
- Pink floral ribbon 20in (50cm)
- White sewing thread

FINISHED SIZE

5½in x 6½in (14cm x 16.5cm) approx.
Use ¼in (5mm) seam allowances unless otherwise stated

WORKING THE ENGLISH PAPER PIECING

1. Trace the hexagon template onto thin card and cut out. Draw round the hexagon onto scrap paper to make twenty-four hexagons and cut them out.

2. Take a paper hexagon and cut a piece of coloured fabric ¼in (5mm) bigger all the way round. Pin the paper to the wrong side of the fabric shape and then fold the fabric round the hexagon and tack (baste) in place (see Basic Techniques: English Paper Piecing). Make the rest of the fabric hexagons in the same way.

3. Lay out the fabric hexagons in four rows each with six hexagons (with the hexagon points upwards) and then sew them all together. Do this by placing two hexagons right sides together and whip stitching the edges together with white sewing thread. Add more hexagons to complete a row. When all rows are sewn, sew the rows together and press well. Remove the paper templates and then trim down to a piece of patchwork 11½in x 5½in (30cm x 14cm).

4. Cut a piece of coordinating fabric 11½in x 2¼in (30cm x 6cm) and sew it to the top of the patchwork (Fig 1).

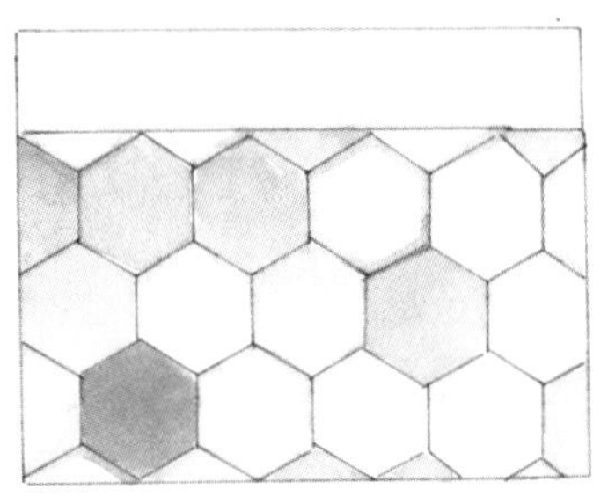

Fig 1

MAKING UP

5. To make a casing for the ribbon, fold over the top of the bag by ¼in (5mm) and then by ½in (1.5cm) and sew in place. Fold over the sides of the patchwork by ¼in (5mm) and sew down ⅛in (3mm) from the edge. Now fold the whole patchwork piece in half, wrong sides together, and sew along the bottom edge and up the side seam, stopping before you get to the casing channel. Fasten off, trim the seams and clip the corners. Turn the bag right side out and press. To finish, thread the length of ribbon through the casing, pull up and tie in a bow (Fig 2).

Fig 2

Template (full size)

Hexagon for paper template
Cut out fabric patches ¼in (5mm) larger all round

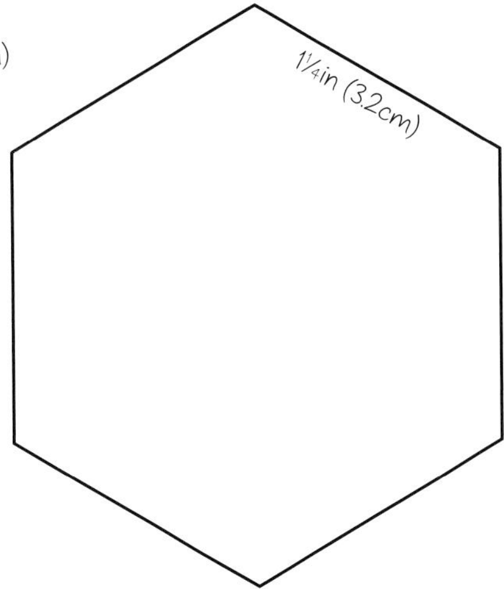

CHRISTMAS WREATH

This decorative wreath is a contemporary take on traditional festive wreaths, using Scandinavian inspired reds, white and pastel blues and greens. It would look lovely against a painted door or on a wall, and you could use the individual elements as tree decorations, too. I have made birds, flowers and candy canes from fabric to decorate my wreath, and added felt balls, holly leaves, bells and buttons for an extra festive look. You could use any other decorations of your choice, either handmade or purchased, to create your own unique design.

You will need

- Polystyrene wreath form 12in (30.5cm) diameter
- Thin card for templates
- Assorted blue and green pastel fabrics, 1yd (1m) in total to wrap wreath
- Red/white striped ribbon for hanging 12in (30.5cm)
- Pink/white spot print for flowers 5in x 11in (12.5cm x 28in)
- Pale green felt for holly leaves, about 5in (12.5cm) square
- Red/white stripe fabric for canes, two 8in (20cm) squares
- Red check and red floral fabric for birds, two pieces of each 6in (15cm) square
- Nine red felt balls for berries and three red felt stars (or use the templates and red felt)
- Red gingham ribbon for bows and two tiny white bows
- Petite seed beads for eyes
- Two white metal bells and one tiny silver bell
- About ten white buttons in assorted sizes
- Glue gun or strong fabric glue

FINISHED SIZE

12in (30.5cm) diameter approx.
Use ¼in (5mm) seam allowances

COVERING THE WREATH

1. Cut the green and blue fabrics into 5in (12.5cm) wide strips of varying lengths. Join together into a strip about 9yds (8.25m) long. Fold in half, wrong sides together and press. Roll it up. Pin the end of the roll to the wrong side of the polystyrene ring with pins (Fig 1). Wind the fabric round until the ring is covered evenly (Fig 2). Secure the end with pins at the back. Secure the striped ribbon at the top back of the wreath with pins.

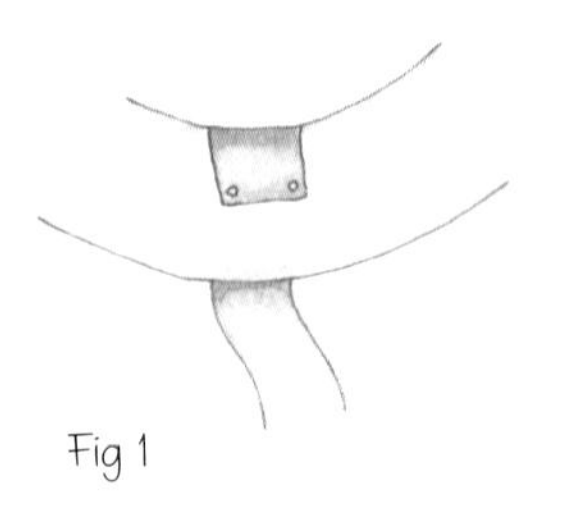

Fig 1

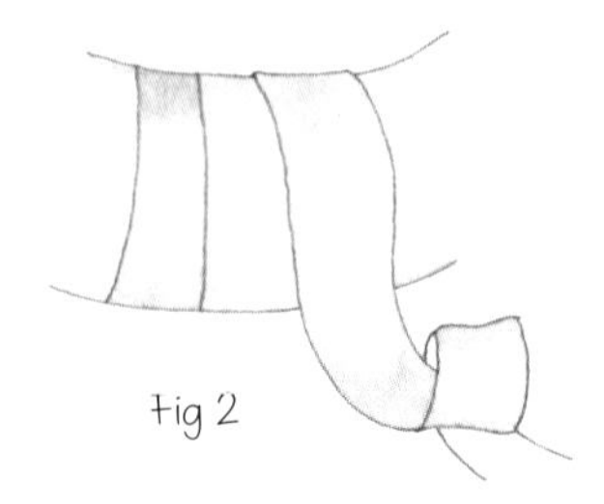

Fig 2

MAKING THE BIRDS

2. There are two birds and they use the same template and sewing process as the Rainbow Birds, so refer to steps 1–3 of that project. Once sewn, sew a tiny white bow on the side of each bird (Fig 3).

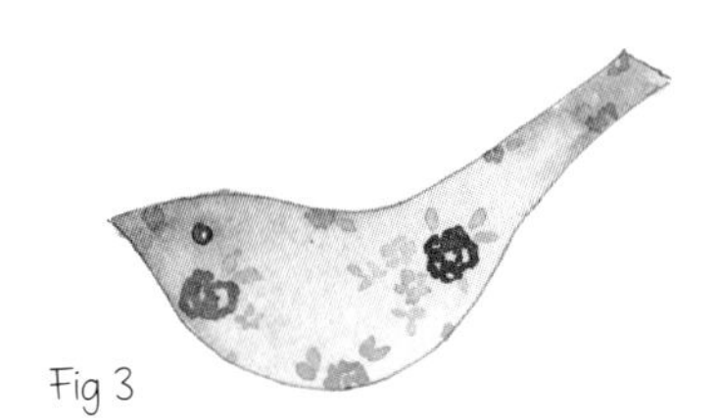

Fig 3

MAKING THE FLOWERS

3. There are two flowers and they use the same template and sewing process as the Strawberry Wreath, so refer to steps 2–3 of that project, using pink/white spot fabric.

MAKING THE CANDY CANES

4. There are three candy canes. Trace the cane template onto thin card and cut out. Put the two pieces of red/white striped fabric right sides together. Draw round the cane three times onto the back of one piece of fabric (Fig 4). Sew round the shape on the line, leaving a gap at the base. Cut out with a ¼in (5mm) seam allowance. Turn through to the right side.

Fig 4

5. Stuff with toy filling, using a knitting needle to push the stuffing to the bottom of the cane. Sew up the gap (Fig 5). Make two more canes like this.

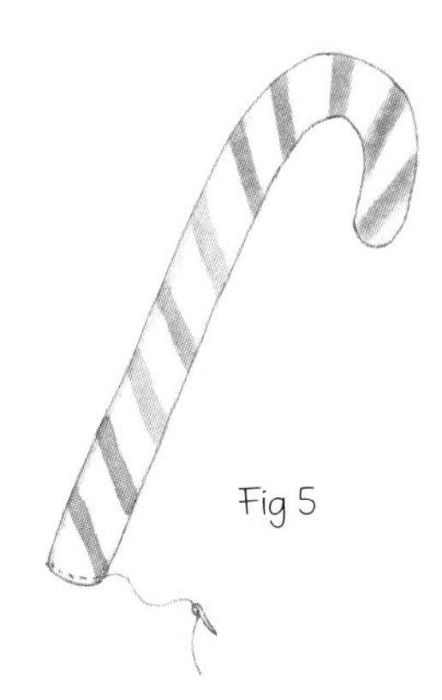

Fig 5

6. With gingham ribbon, tie two canes together, (facing opposite directions). Tie ribbon round the single cane and add a silver bell.

MAKING THE HOLLY

7. Trace the holly leaf template onto thin card and cut out. Draw round the leaf shape on pale green felt to make eight leaves and cut out.

ASSEMBLING THE WREATH

8. Refer to the main photo. Tie two white bells together with ribbon and tie near the top of the wreath. Glue a bird to each side of the wreath. Add the candy canes. Pin the holly leaves in place and glue red felt balls on top. Glue the flowers in place. Add the red felt stars, with white button centres. (If not using ready-cut stars, use the template and red felt to make them.) Finally, glue on a few white buttons in places around the wreath.

Templates (full size)

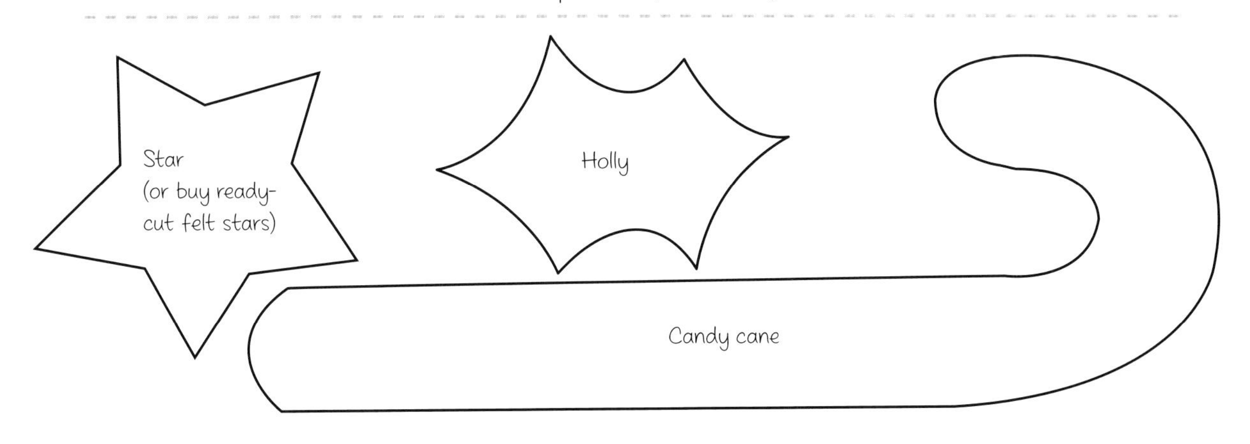

BUTTERFLY GIFT TAGS

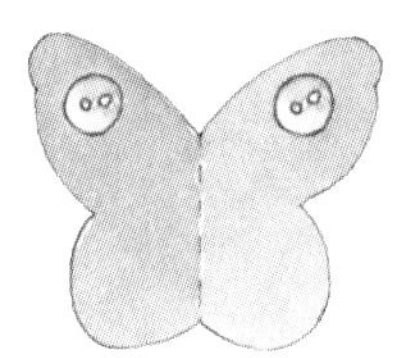

These little fluttering butterfly tags are easy and fun to create and add a really special touch when attached to any gift. They are a great way to use up lots of favourite scraps that are just too small for other projects. You can use any patterned fabric or papers to create your own tags and make them as colourful as you wish.

For one tag

- White card
- Gingham-patterned paper
- Spotted fabric 5½in x 2¾in (14cm x 7cm)
- Fusible web
- White and blue sewing threads
- Narrow ribbon
- Coloured eyelets (optional)
- Two tiny coloured buttons
- Hot glue gun or strong fabric glue
- Baker's twine

FINISHED SIZE

2in x 4in (5cm x 10cm) approx. Use ¼in (5mm) seam allowances

MAKING THE TAG

1. Cut a tag 4in x 2in (10cm x 5cm) from white card. Cover the front of the tag with gingham-patterned paper (Fig 1). Punch a hole in the top centre and set in a coloured eyelet, if you wish. Glue a piece of ribbon to the front, about halfway down.

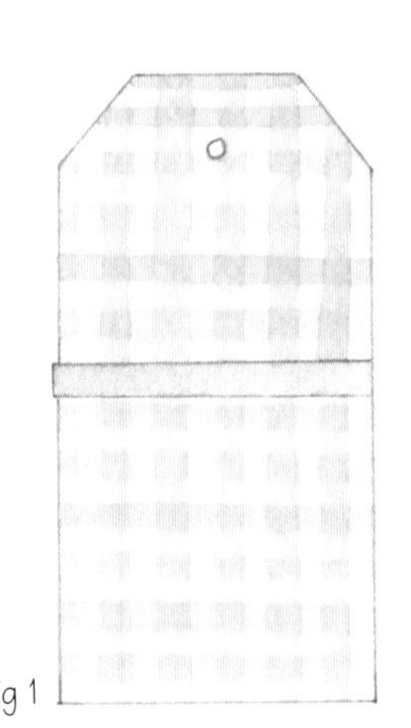

Fig 1

tip

You could use butterflies to embellish other projects, perhaps adding one or more to a cushion, or to create a fabric picture.

ADDING THE BUTTERFLY

2. Trace the butterfly template onto white card and cut out. Take the piece of spotted fabric and iron fusible web onto the back (Fig 2). Peel off the paper backing and fold the fabric in half, so the web on both halves is facing. Press the fabric again, fusing the two sides together.

3. Draw round the butterfly template on one side of the fused fabric – this will be the back of the butterfly (Fig 3). Cut out the shape carefully. Sew a line of running stitch around the outer edge of the butterfly using white sewing thread.

Fig 2

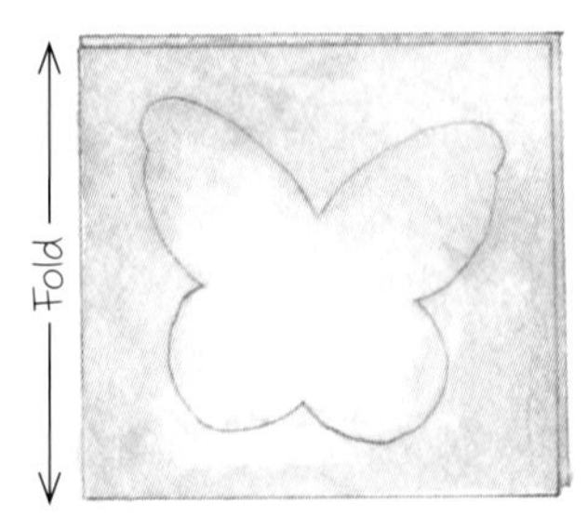

Fig 3

4. Fold the butterfly in half and press so there is a crease down the centre where the butterfly body would be. Sew a line of blue thread along the crease using long stitch. Sew two tiny buttons to the top wings using white thread (Fig 4).

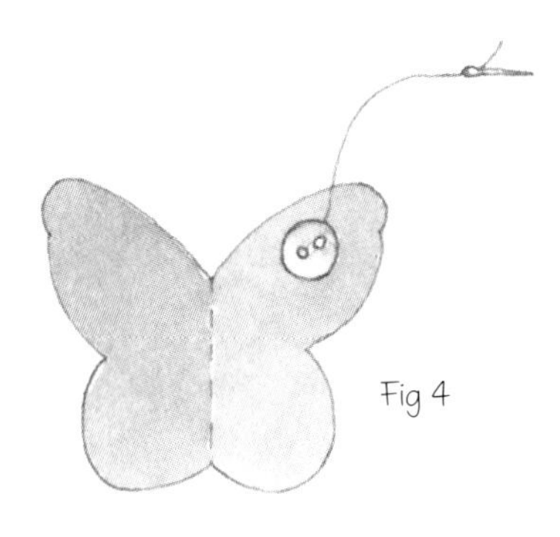

FINISHING OFF

5. Glue the butterfly in the centre of the tag, over the top of the ribbon and at a slight angle, using a hot glue gun or strong fabric glue – only securing part of the butterfly so it can still 'flutter' a little. Finally, tie a piece of baker's twine through the eyelet hole and knot neatly.

Template (full size)

BUTTON HOUSES

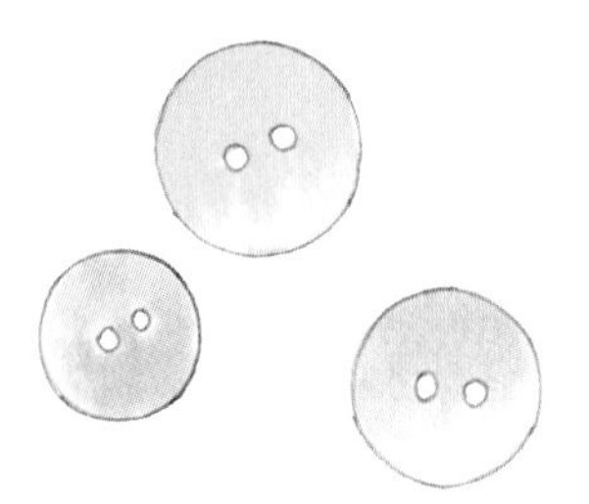

This project is so simple yet it is one of my favourites because it is cute, versatile and uses lots of scraps of pretty fabrics. I have made a collection of little button houses into a garland, and love them just dotted about the house looking colourful and decorative. They would make lovely Christmas tree decorations, or a sweet little key fob for a house-warming gift.

You will need

For one house

- Patterned fabric for house 3in x 8in (7.5cm x 20cm)
- Contrast fabric for roof 3in x 2in (7.5cm x 5cm)
- Scrap of fabric for door
- Fusible web
- Polyester toy filling
- Narrow ribbon about 2¼in (5.5cm) long
- White or pastel sewing thread
- Thin card for templates
- Small button

XXXXXXXXXXXXXXXXXXXXXX

FINISHED SIZE

2in x 4in (5cm x 10cm) approx. Use ¼in (5mm) seam allowances

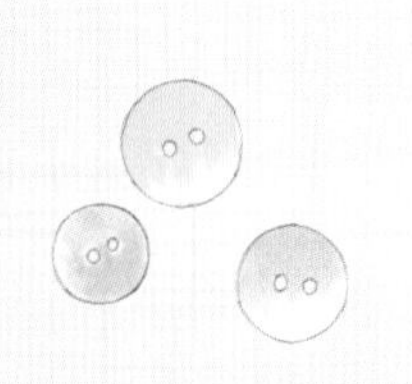

MAKING THE HOUSE

1. Cut a piece of patterned fabric for the back of the house 4in x 2½in (10cm x 6.5cm). Cut a piece of the same patterned fabric for the front of the house 3in x 2½in (7.5cm x 6.5cm). Cut a contrasting piece of fabric for the roof 1½in x 2½in (4cm x 6.5cm). Sew the roof fabric to the front of the house and press the seam (Fig 1).

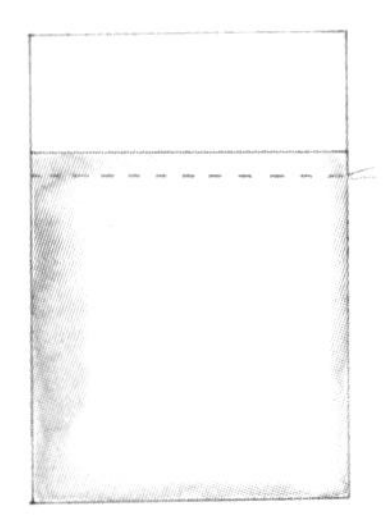
Fig 1

2. Trace the house/roof template onto thin card and cut out. Place the template on the wrong side of the front of the house/roof fabric, align the roof line with the seam and draw round the template (Fig 2).

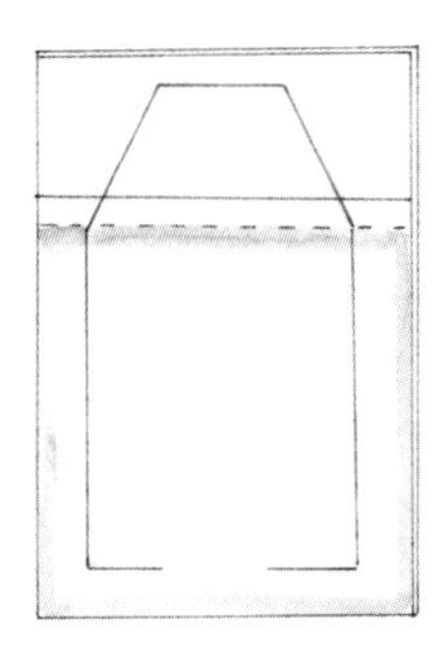
Fig 2

3. Pin a piece of narrow ribbon to the top centre of the roof so it lies on the right side, pointing downwards. Take the house back piece and with right sides together sew round the house shape, leaving a small gap at the bottom for turning (Fig 3). Trim the seams and clip the bottom corners. Turn the right way out and press. Stuff the house with toy stuffing and then sew up the gap neatly.

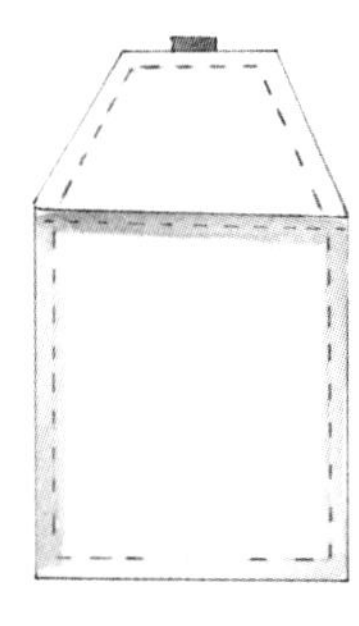
Fig 3

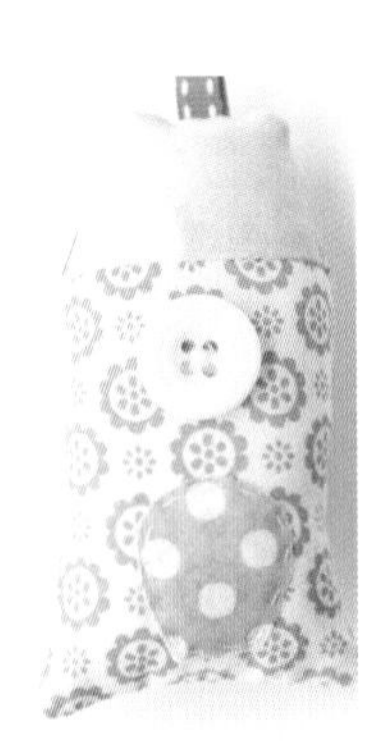

ADDING THE DETAILS

4. For the door, take a small scrap of contrasting fabric and iron fusible web on the back. Trace the door template onto the paper side of the web and cut out. Peel off the paper, place the door on the front of the house and fuse in place with an iron. Stitch round the door with white or pastel thread and running stitch. Finally, sew on a button as a window (Fig 4).

Fig 4

tip

You could use Christmas-themed fabrics to create a novel set of houses for festive tree decorations.

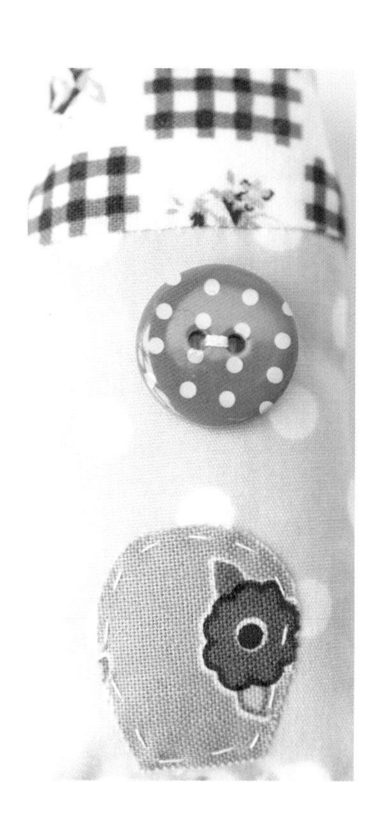

Templates (full size)

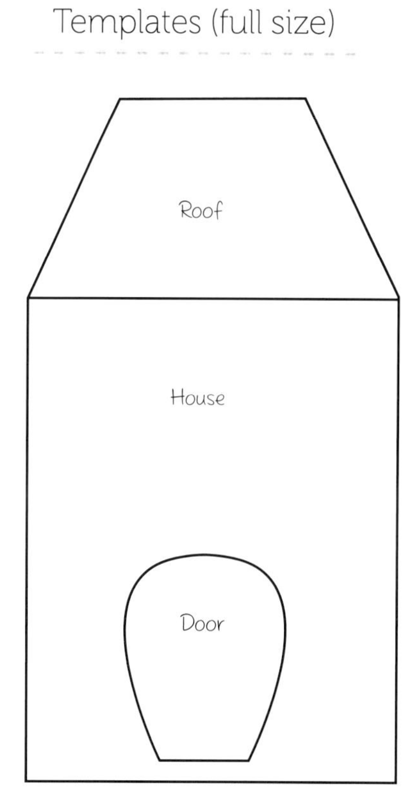

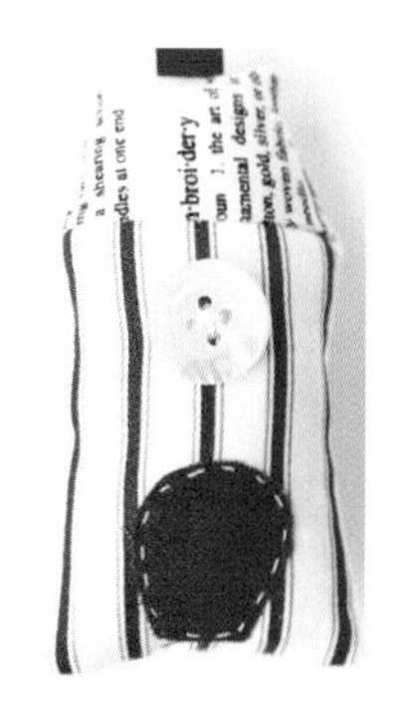

HOLLY COASTERS

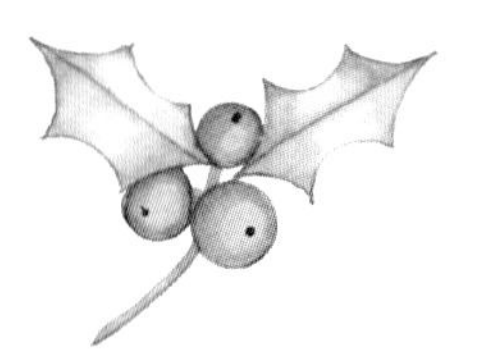

A quick and fun little make, these holly coasters are modern, festive and very useful. You can make just one to accompany a new mug or cup and saucer for a special gift, or create a whole set, tied together with red and white baker's twine or Christmas ribbon. The fabrics used can be fresh and modern or more traditional and festive.

NOËL

You will need

For each coaster

- Two pieces of aqua print fabric 4½in (11.5cm) square
- Lightweight wadding (batting) 4in (10cm) square
- Scrap of red spotty fabric
- Scrap of green fabric
- Fusible web
- White sewing thread
- Red and green embroidery cotton (floss)
- Thin card for templates
- Red/white baker's twine (optional)

For the tag (optional)

- Scraps of card in white, red and aqua
- Red ric-rac 8in (20cm) long
- Word rubber stamp and red ink pad (I used 'Noel')

FINISHED SIZE

4in (10cm) square approx.
Use ¼in (5mm) seam allowances

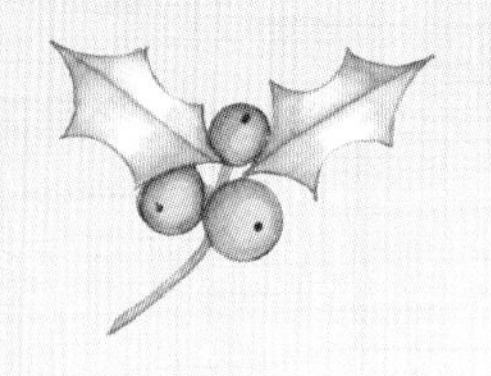

WORKING THE APPLIQUÉ

1. Trace the holly leaves and the berry shapes onto thin card and cut out carefully. Iron fusible web onto the back of the red and green fabrics. Draw round the two holly leaf shapes on the back of the green fabric (Fig 1). Draw round the holly berry shape twice (for each coaster) on the back of the red fabric (Fig 2).

Fig 1

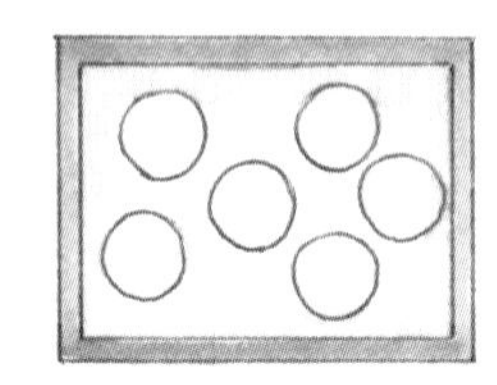

Fig 2

2. Carefully cut out the holly leaves and the berries and place them on the front piece of fabric for the coaster. When you are happy with the arrangement, peel the backing paper from the web and iron the shapes in place. Using green embroidery cotton (floss) sew a running stitch round the leaves, and using red cotton do the same round the berries.

MAKING UP THE COASTER

3. Take the front and back pieces, and with right sides together, sew round the edge with a ¼in (5mm) seam, leaving a gap at the bottom (Fig 3). Trim seams, clip corners and turn to the right side. Push out the corners.

4 Place the piece of wadding (batting) inside the coaster and smooth it out – it's fiddly but does work. When the wadding is arranged inside the coaster sew the gap closed and then press.

5. Quilt round the holly shapes and along the edges of the coaster. Quilt a square behind the holly design in the centre of the coaster (Fig 4). Make more coasters in the same way.

Fig 3

Fig 4

MAKING A TAG

6. When you have made several coaters, tie them together with baker's twine. If desired, add a rubber-stamped tag, as follows. Print the word of your choice onto a piece of white card using the red ink pad and rubber stamp. Cut out the stamped word close to the edge and mount on red card.

7. Cut a tag shape from aqua card, big enough to leave a border around the word. Attach the word to the front of the tag. Punch a hole at the top of the tag and tie a piece of red ric-rac through to finish.

Templates (full size)

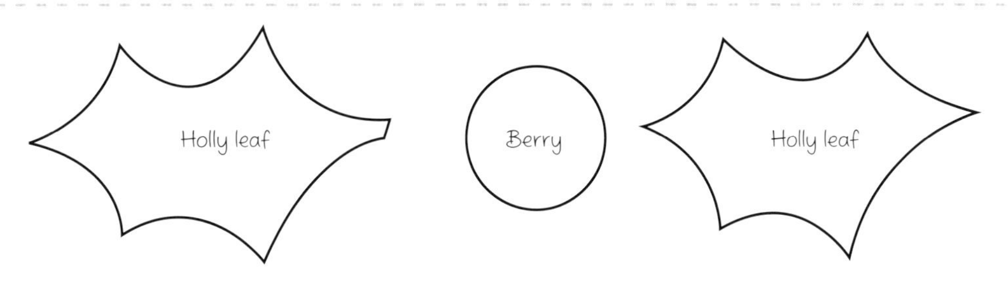

LITTLE DOG DOLL'S QUILT

This little quilt is simple to make and has a modern look with its graphic image of a small terrier appliquéd onto a background of striped and spotted patchwork squares. Small children love animal themes and they also enjoy tucking up their toys in bed, so they are sure to enjoy using this tiny quilt.

You will need

- Pink striped fabric ⅛yd (0.125m)
- Grey/white polka dot fabric ⅛yd (0.125m)
- Solid black fabric for dog appliqués ⅛yd (0.125m)
- Thin card for template
- Fusible web
- Aqua/pink polka dot fabric for backing, about 14in x 17in (35.5cm x 43cm)
- Wadding (batting), about 14in x 17in (35.5cm x 43cm)
- Black and white ticking fabric for binding ⅛yd (0.125m)
- DMC Color Variations cotton (floss) in aqua
- Black and white sewing thread
- Nine tiny blue bows and one tiny pink bow
- One decorative button

FINISHED SIZE

12in x 15in (30.5cm x 38cm) approx.
Use ¼in (5mm) seam allowances unless otherwise stated

MAKING THE DOG APPLIQUÉS

1. Trace the dog template onto thin card. Iron fusible web onto the back of the black fabric and then draw round the dog template ten times, reversing (flipping) the template so that four of the dogs face in the opposite direction (Fig 1). Cut out the dog appliqués and set aside for the moment.

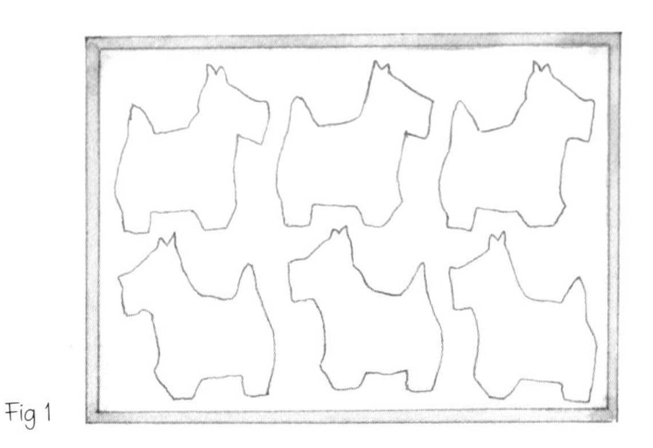

Fig 1

MAKING THE QUILT

2. Cut out ten 3½in (9cm) squares from pink striped fabric and ten 3½in (9cm) squares from the grey/white polka dot fabric. Place the squares alternately, changing the direction of the stripes on alternate rows. Sew together into five rows each with four squares. Join the rows, matching up seams neatly and pinning the corners of the squares for accuracy.

3. When the squares are all sewn together, take the dog appliqués and place them in the centres of the grey/white polka dot squares. When you are happy with the placement, and the direction each dog is facing, peel off the fusible web paper and iron the appliqués in place (Fig 2). Using black sewing thread, sew round the dog shapes with blanket stitch (see Basic Techniques: Stitches).

Fig 2

QUILTING AND FINISHING

4. Take the backing fabric, wadding (batting) and quilt and layer together in a quilt sandwich – see Basic Techniques: Making a Quilt Sandwich. Using two strands of aqua embroidery cotton (floss) and starting in the centre, quilt along three seams from top to bottom, and four seams from side to side. Using white sewing thread, quilt round the dogs and a small circle in the centre of each striped square.

5. Cut two 2¼in (5.5cm) x width of fabric strips of binding fabric and sew together. Fold in half, wrong sides together, and press. Bind the quilt, mitring corners neatly (Fig 3). See Basic Techniques: Binding.

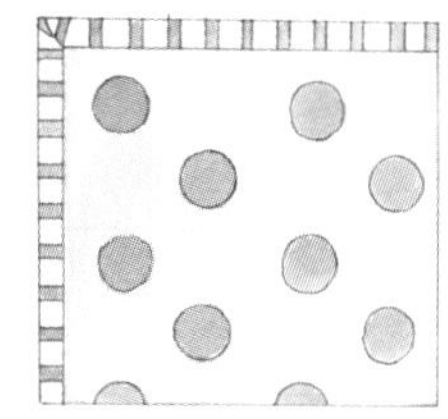

Fig 3

6. Finally, sew the tiny bows onto the dogs, and add a button or two if you wish.

tip

You could stitch just one of the tiny terriers onto a square of fabric to make a card or a decorative hanger.

Template (full size)

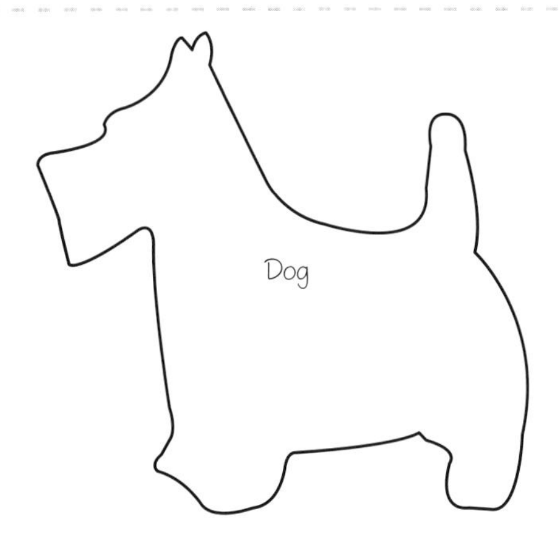

TUMBLER PATCHWORK PILLOW

The traditional tumbler patchwork shape can be used in scrappy quilts of all sizes and always looks effective. This English paper-pieced pattern uses red and white tumblers for a contemporary style. The tumblers work well in a horizontal arrangement so I decided to make an oblong sofa pillow, decorated with small red bows at the top. This pillow looks lovely made as a companion to the Tumbler Flowerpot Pillow.

You will need

- Thin card for template
- Scrap paper for templates
- White cotton fabric, fat quarter
- Assorted red/white cotton fabrics, total of a fat quarter or about 4in (10cm) square of each
- Red spotted fabric for backing 21½in x 12in (55cm x 30.5cm)
- Sewing threads to suit fabrics
- Red ribbon about 2yd (2m) for ties
- Cushion pad 22in x 12in (56cm x 30.5cm)

XXXXXXXXXXXXXXXXXXXXXX

FINISHED SIZE

21in x 11½in (55cm x 30cm) approx.
Use ¼in (5mm) seam allowances unless otherwise stated

PREPARING THE TUMBLER SHAPES

1. Trace the tumbler template onto thin card and cut out. Draw round the tumbler template onto scrap paper to make thirty-six shapes.

2. Choose a selection of red/ white fabrics and cut out eighteen tumbler shapes using the template as a guide, adding a ¼in (5mm) seam allowance all round. Now cut out eighteen white fabric tumbler shapes.

3. To create the tumbler patchwork pieces, pin one paper tumbler on the wrong side of one fabric tumbler (Fig 1). Fold the fabric seam allowance round the shape neatly and tack (baste) in place (Fig 2). Prepare the remaining tumbler patchwork pieces in the same way.

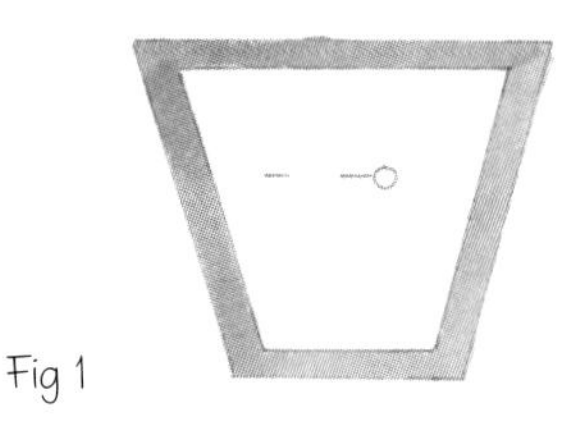

Fig 1

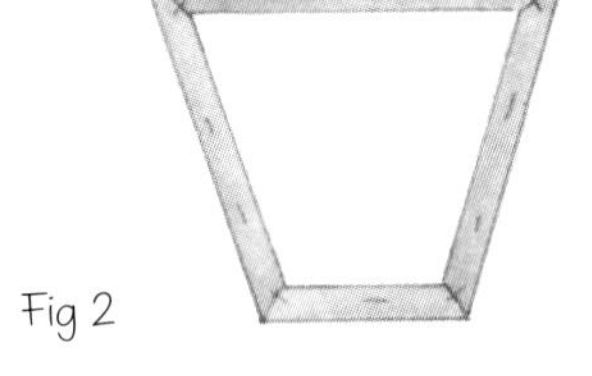

Fig 2

tip

If cutting out tumbler shapes from a single piece of fabric, rotate the tumbler shape alternately on the fabric for the most economical cuts. Remember to allow for a seam allowance.

ASSEMBLING THE PATCHWORK

4. Sew the fabric tumblers together in four rows each with nine shapes and alternating the red/white and plain white colours. To do this, place two tumblers right sides together and sew together using whipstitch. Add another tumbler, rotating as necessary, until a row is complete. When you have sewn four rows, join them together along the long edge. Remove the papers and press the patchwork flat. Trim the patchwork to 21½in x 12in (55cm x 30.5cm), or so that half tumblers are created at either end of the patchwork.

MAKING UP

5. To make up the pillow, pin the backing fabric right sides together with the patchwork. Starting about 2in (5cm) away from the top right corner and using a 3/8in (1cm) seam, sew together all round, stopping about 2in (5cm) past the final corner, so leaving a long gap along the top of the pillow. Trim seams, clip corners, turn right way out and push out the corners. Press the pillow and turn in each raw edge of the opening neatly and press.

6. Cut four lengths of ribbon, each about 18in (45cm) long and then cut each piece into two equal lengths. Pin the ribbon lengths to the pillow, spacing them equally along the gap, with one piece on either side of the gap on the inside of the pressed edge. Hand sew them in place. Place the cushion pad inside and tie the ribbons at the top closed (Fig 3). For a non-standard shape of pad it is best to make your own – see Basic Techniques: Making a Cushion Pad.

Fig 3

Template (full size)

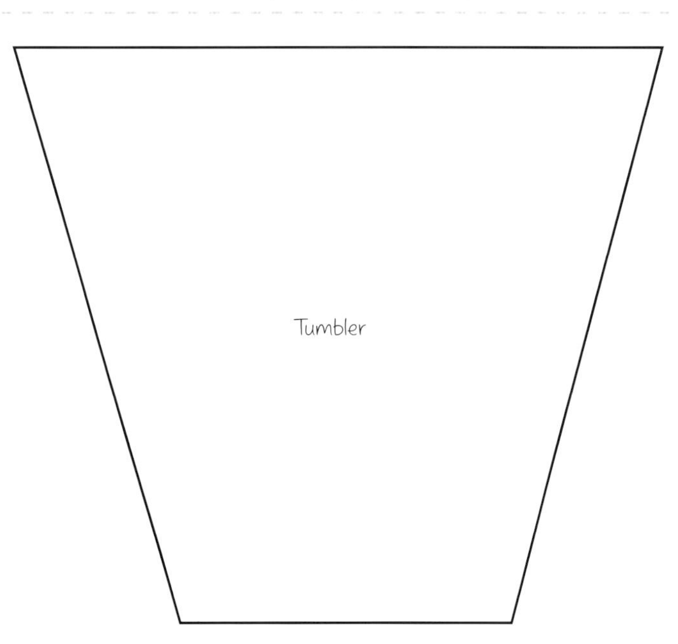

TUMBLER FLOWERPOT PILLOW

This modern red and white design was inspired by the traditional tumbler patchwork shape which, of course, makes a perfect flowerpot, so I decided to explore this idea and add some simple appliqué plants. You can use any red and white prints for the pots and appliqué leaves, or change the look completely by using other colours.

You will need

- Thin card for template
- Scrap paper for templates
- White fabric ¼yd (0.25m)
- Scraps of red/white print fabrics for pots and appliqué, about fat quarter in total
- Red/white striped fabric ⅛yd (0.125m)
- Red/white patterned print for pillow back, two pieces each 10in x 15½in (25.5cm x 40cm)
- Fusible web
- Red sewing thread
- Cushion pad 15in (38cm) square
- Two white buttons for cushion back (optional)

FINISHED SIZE

15in (40cm) square approx. Use ¼in (5mm) seam allowances

PREPARING THE TUMBLER SHAPES

1. Trace the tumbler template (see the Tumbler Patchwork Pillow project) onto thin card and cut out. Draw round the template onto scrap paper seven times.

2. Choose three red/white fabrics and cut out using the tumbler template, adding a ¼in (5mm) seam allowance all round. Cut out four white fabric tumblers.

3. To create the tumbler patchwork pieces, pin one paper tumbler on the wrong side of one fabric tumbler. Fold the fabric round the shape neatly and tack (baste) in place. Prepare the remaining tumbler patchwork pieces in the same way.

PIECING THE PILLOW FRONT

4. Sew the fabric tumblers together as shown in Fig 1, to form a strip. Fold the last tumbler shape at either end of the strip inwards to form a straight edge.

5. Cut a strip of white fabric 2¼in x 15½in (6cm x 40cm) and sew to the bottom of the tumbler strip. Cut white fabric 4¼in x 15½in (11cm x 40cm) and sew to the top edge of the tumbler strip. Press the pillow front.

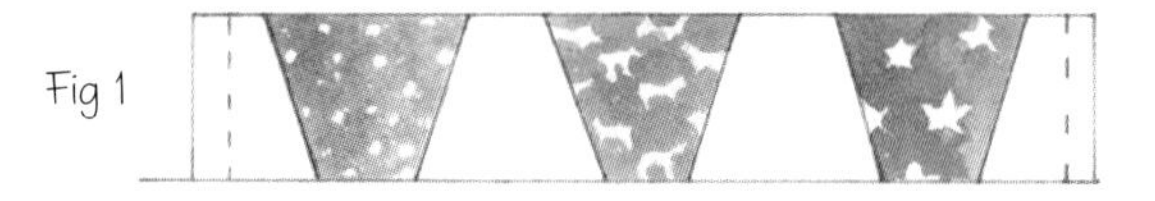

Fig 1

ADDING THE APPLIQUÉ

6. Take a piece of red/white print and iron fusible web on the back. Trace the seven-leaf arrangement onto thin card and cut out. Draw round the leaves on the back of the web-backed fabric (Fig 2). Cut out the leaves carefully. Repeat for the other two pots.

7. Position the leaves above the flowerpots and when you are happy with the arrangement, peel off the papers and iron the leaves in place. Sew round each leaf using red thread and blanket stitch.

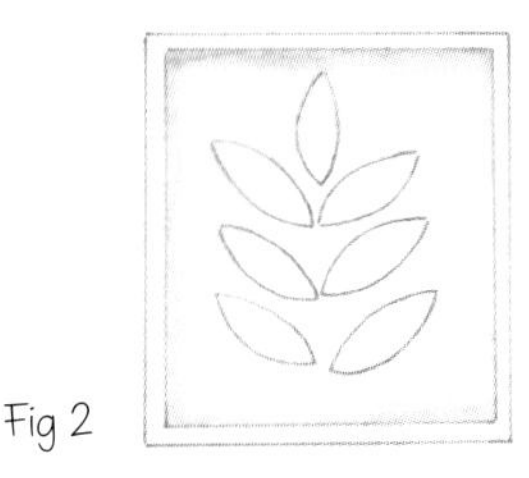

Fig 2

ADDING THE STRIPED BORDERS

8. Cut two borders from red/ white stripe, each 3¼in x 15½in (8.5cm x 40cm) and sew to the top and bottom edge of the patchwork (Fig 3).

Fig 3

MAKING UP

9. To make the back, take the two 10in x 15½in (25.5cm x 40cm) pieces of red/white print. On one long edge of each piece fold over a hem, press and sew. Place the front right side up and the backing pieces on top, right side down and aligning all outer edges. They will overlap in the centre. Pin the back pieces together on the overlap. Sew around the outside edge with a ¼in (5mm) seam allowance.

10. Trim the seams and clip the corners. Remove the pins, turn the cover right way out, pushing out the corners and press. Insert the cushion pad. Sew two white buttons on the back if you wish.

Template (full size)

Use the tumbler template supplied with the Tumbler Patchwork Pillow project

BIG BUTTON QUILT

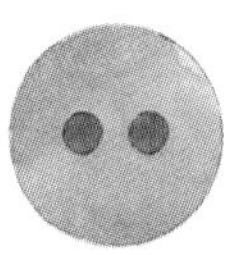

Most crafters use, collect and actually love buttons, so here is a quick little quilt featuring some big appliqué buttons. To keep it simple and fresh I chose just one of my favourite prints for the squares and alternated them with white squares. For the buttons I used solid fabrics in a variety of colours, just like the buttons in my button jar. It is a contemporary design but could also be made with a mix of different fabrics for a scrappier look.

You will need

- Eighteen coloured print 6in (15cm) squares
- Seventeen white 6in (15cm) squares
- Seventeen 4in (10cm) solid coloured fabrics for large circles for buttons
- Scraps of solid black fabric for thirty-four small circles for buttonholes
- Fusible web
- Pink fabric for border ½yd (0.5m)
- Lightweight wadding (batting) about 40in x 44in (102cm x 112cm)
- Backing fabric about 40in x 44in (102cm x 112cm)
- Black/white striped binding fabric ¼yd (0.25m)
- Grey and black sewing thread

FINISHED SIZE

34½in x 40in (88cm x 102cm) approx.
Use ¼in (5mm) seam allowances unless otherwise stated

PIECING THE QUILT

1. Sew all the squares together alternately into six rows, each with five squares (see photo). Press the seams in alternate rows in opposite directions, so they will 'nest' together neatly. Now sew the rows together, matching seams neatly. Press the quilt.

2. From the pink border fabric cut two strips 4in x 28in (10cm x 71cm) (or long enough to fit *your* quilt). Sew these to the top and bottom of the quilt and press the seams outwards. Cut two strips of border fabric 4in x 40½in (10cm x 103cm) (or long enough to fit your quilt). Sew these to the sides of the quilt and press the seams outwards.

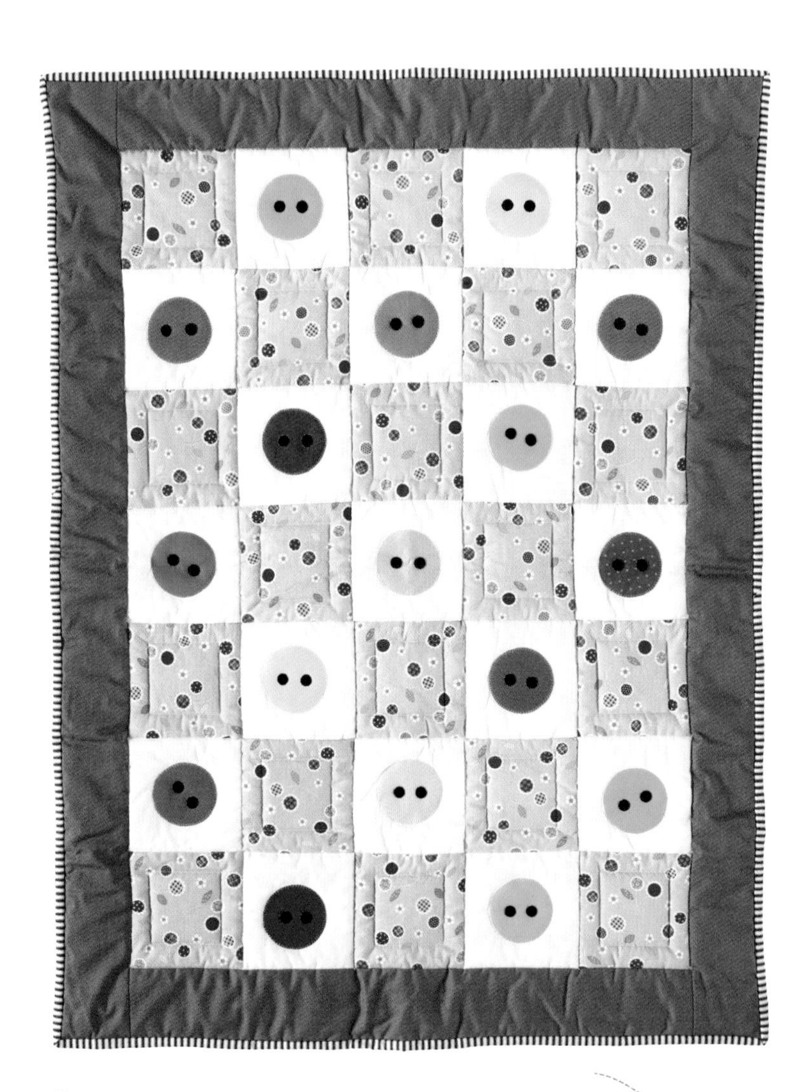

tip

You could create a matching cushion by making just a few blocks, or a nine-patch arrangement, and sewing them to a plain background. Refer to the Mushroom Pillow project for making up a cushion.

ADDING THE APPLIQUÉ

3. Iron fusible web onto the back of the solid colour fabrics and trace the large circle for the buttons onto the paper side of the web seventeen times. Cut out the circles. Trace the tiny circles for the buttonholes onto the black solid fabric thirty-four times and cut out.

4. Iron the large coloured circles onto the white squares one by one and sew round with grey sewing thread and blanket stitch (Fig 1). Iron on the tiny black circles in the button centres and sew round them with blanket stitch and black sewing thread (Fig 2).

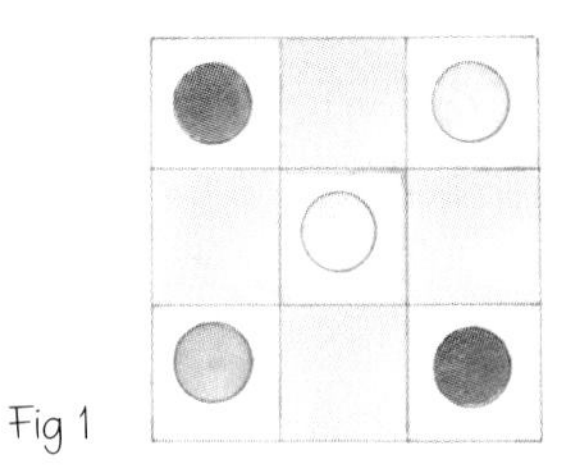

Fig 1

Fig 2

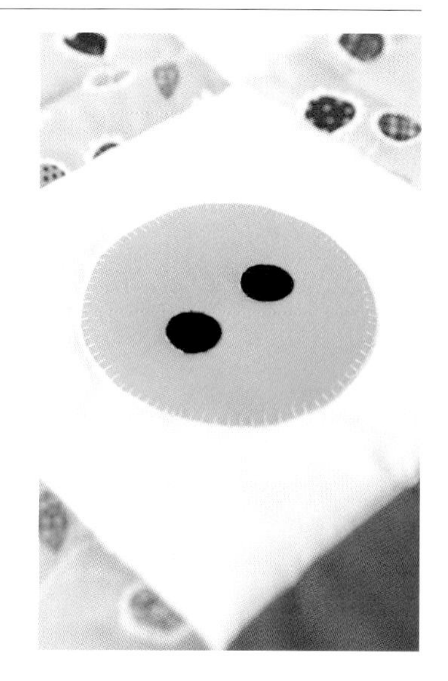

QUILTING AND FINISHING

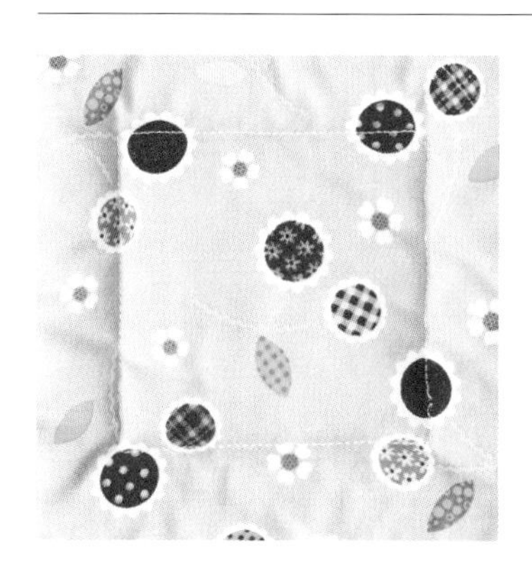

5. Take the backing fabric, wadding (batting) and quilt top and layer together in a quilt sandwich (see Basic Techniques: Making a Quilt Sandwich). Quilt the design in your choice of pattern – I quilted in the seam ditches and a simple grid pattern in the coloured squares.

6. Cut four 2¼in (5.5cm) x width of fabric strips of binding fabric and sew them together. Fold in half along the length, wrong sides together, and press. Add the binding to the quilt as described in Basic Techniques: Binding, mitring the corners neatly. Press to finish.

Templates (full size)

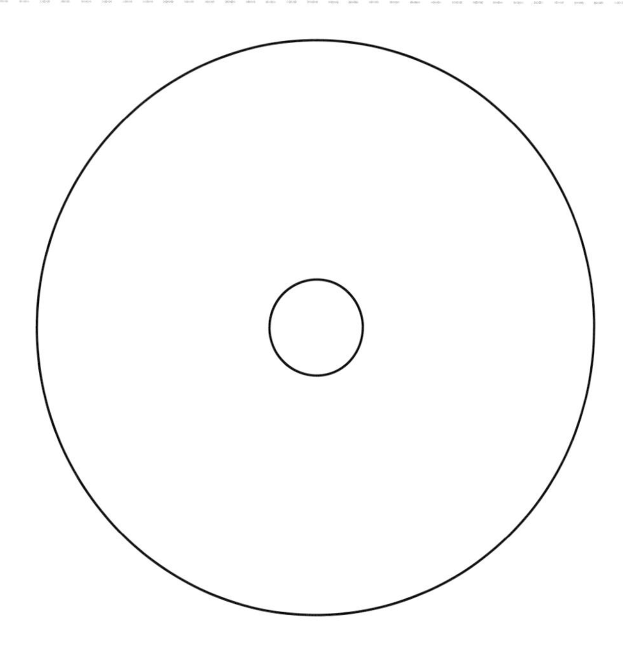

MATERIALS & EQUIPMENT

This section will be useful for beginners as it contains information on the materials and equipment you will need to work the projects in the book.

FABRICS

Most of the projects are sewn with lovely printed cottons in fresh and contemporary colours and patterns. In most cases seam allowances have been included, but check the project instructions. Seam allowances for patchwork piecing are usually ¼in (5mm). When sewing, check that your seam allowance is accurate as this will help the patchwork pieces fit together accurately. Some projects use felt, which doesn't require a seam as it does not fray.

Spend a little time preparing the fabric before stitching to save time in the long run.

- Before beginning to stitch it is a good idea to neaten the fabric edges, removing the selvedges. Check the fabric is squared up (right angled).
- Press all fabrics before use.
- If you think a fabric may not be colourfast then wash, dry and iron it before use.

WADDING (BATTING)

Wadding is used for padding and to give an attractive puffy look when quilted. There are various types of wadding available, including cotton and polyester. For the projects in this book choose a thin wadding that is easily sewn through. In most cases only small pieces of wadding are needed.

THREADS

You will need hand and machine sewing and quilting threads for the projects in this book, in colours to match your fabrics. Some projects are embellished with DMC stranded embroidery cotton (floss), which is available as six-stranded skeins that can be split into separate strands. In general for the projects use one strand of thread for blanket stitch appliqué and working embroidery stitches.

CARD AND PAPER

Thin card and scrap paper will be needed to create templates for the projects. Use card for master templates – a similar weight to cereal packet card will do. Use scrap paper to create as many templates as you need for English paper piecing. Remember to cut out all templates accurately.

FUSIBLE WEB

This is a very useful product with a glue web on both sides, which allows you to fuse one fabric to another – perfect for appliqué. There are various brands available, such as Bondaweb (also called Vliesofix and Wonder Under) and Steam-A-Seam. Use a medium-hot iron and refer to the manufacturer's instructions.

EMBELLISHMENTS

Various embellishments have been used on the projects, including buttons, beads, ribbons, bows and braids. Your local craft store should have a good selection and see Suppliers for useful addresses.

MEASURING AND CUTTING TOOLS

For patchwork it is best to use a quilter's ruler, rotary cutter and self-healing mat to measure and cut out fabrics quickly and accurately. A 6in x 18in ruler and a 45mm diameter rotary cutter will be most helpful. An ordinary tape measure and a sharp pair of scissors will also be useful.

PINS AND NEEDLES

Dressmaking pins will be needed for patchwork piecing and perhaps safety pins for making a quilt sandwich – curved pins are useful for this. Standard hand sewing and machine sewing needles will be needed to create the projects. Glass seed beads are used on some of the projects and you will need a thinner beading needle to attach these.

FABRIC MARKERS

You will need to be able to mark designs and shapes on fabric for some projects and there are many types of markers available for this. It is best to use a removable marker and this may be an air-erasable marker that fades after a period of time, a water-soluble marker, which can be removed with a light spray of water, or a simple chalk marker. Always test a marker on scrap fabric first.

GLUE

Glue is used on some of the projects to fix pieces in place, for example the Christmas Wreath. You could use a strong fabric glue or a hot glue gun, which is fast and effective.

SEWING MACHINE AND IRON

A basic sewing machine and standard iron will be fine for the projects in this book.

BASIC TECHNIQUES

The projects give specific instructions on the techniques used, while this section describes more general techniques needed.

USING TEMPLATES

Templates are provided full size for the projects, at the end of the project instructions. To use a template trace the outline onto thin card or thick paper and cut out the shape carefully. Place the shape on your fabric and draw round it. If no seam allowance is needed, cut out the fabric shape on the drawn line. If the fabric needs a seam allowance then cut out the shape further out, usually ¼in (5mm) all round. If making paper templates for English paper piecing, then copy the shape onto scrap paper as many times as needed.

FUSIBLE WEB APPLIQUÉ

Appliqué is a technique where one fabric is attached to another, with the top fabric usually cut to a shape. Many of the projects use appliqué and it's really easy with fusible web, which has a glue web on both sides.

1. Draw the shape on the paper backing of the fusible web and roughly cut out the shape.

2. Place your appliqué fabric right side down and place the fusible web shape on top of the fabric, glue side down. Iron with a medium iron to fuse it to the fabric. Cut out the shape following your drawn line.

3. Peel off the backing paper and place the patch right side up on the right side of the background fabric and fuse into place. The edges of the appliqué can be further secured with stitches, including blanket stitch, large straight stitches, running stitch or machine satin stitch.

ENGLISH PAPER PIECING

Many of the projects use this technique, which is very simple to do and highly portable, so you can sew anywhere. It can be worked with many shapes, including hexagons, triangles and diamonds.

1. Create a master template of the shape using thin card. Use this master template to cut more shapes from paper, as many as specified in the project instructions. These shapes can be re-used.

2. Cut out the fabric shapes ¼in (5mm) bigger all round than the paper templates, to allow for a seam allowance. If you wish, you could create another master template that is the correct size for the fabric shape. Depending on the shape being used you should be able to rotate the shape alternately on the fabric, to get the most economical cuts.

3. Pin a paper shape in the middle of a fabric shape, with the fabric wrong side up (see Fig 1 for two examples). Fold the edges of the fabric shape carefully over the edges of the paper shape and tack (baste) in place. Press firmly. Repeat with the other fabric shapes.

4. Sew shapes together in the pattern shown in the project, using matching sewing thread and whip stitch (Fig 2). When possible, try to join shapes so they create separate sections with straight edges, to make it easier to join sections together. Press the finished patchwork and remove the paper.

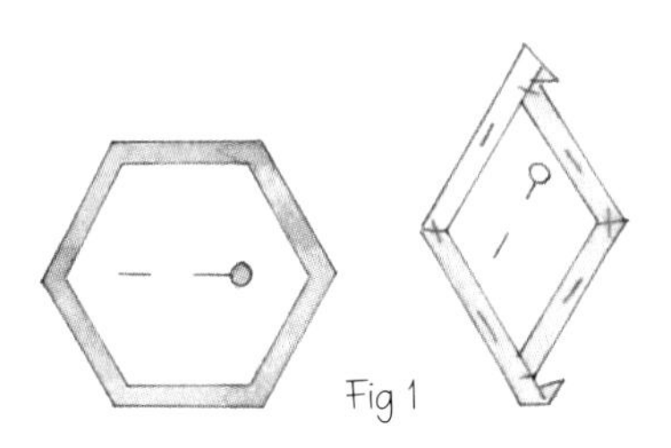
Fig 1

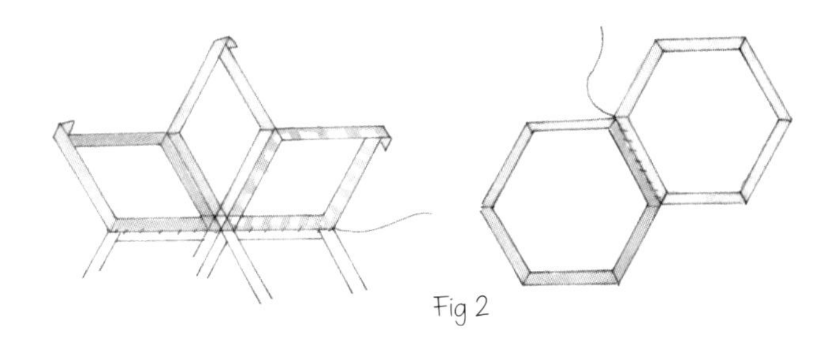
Fig 2

MAKING A CUSHION PAD

Commercially, cushion pads tend to come in a limited range of sizes but it's really easy to make your own in any size you wish. You can use an inexpensive fabric for the pad, such as calico.

1. Cut two pieces of fabric about ¼in (5mm) larger all round than the size of pad you need. Place the pieces right sides together and sew round the edge using a ¼in (5mm) seam, and leaving a gap for turning through.

2. Turn the pad through to the right side, push out the corners and then stuff the pad with polyester toy filling. Stitch the gap closed neatly and your pad is ready.

MAKING A YO-YO

Yo-yos make attractive embellishments and can be used on all sorts of projects, especially if you want a three-dimensional look.

1. Start with a circle of fabric twice the size that you want the finished yo-yo to be. Fold the edges over all round by ¼in (5mm) and use strong sewing thread to make a running stitch all round this folded edge (Fig 3A).

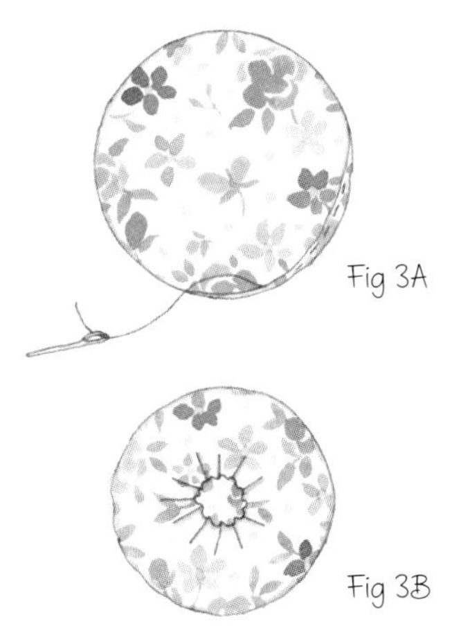
Fig 3A

Fig 3B

2 Pull the thread up and gather the fabric so only a small gap remains. Secure the thread. Arrange the gathers and press the yo-yo (Fig 3B). The yo-yo can then be attached to a fabric base, gathered side up, with slipstitches. You could add a button or bead or some decorative stitches, such as French knots, in the centre if you wish.

MAKING A QUILT SANDWICH

When a project is quilted, a quilt 'sandwich' is created to give a nice, padded look.

1. Cut the backing fabric and wadding (batting) at least 2in (5cm) bigger than the quilt all round (or a little less if the quilt is very small).

2. Place your pressed backing fabric right side down on a flat surface. Place the wadding on top and smooth out. Place the pressed top fabric or patchwork right side up on top of this. Secure these three layers together: this can be done in various ways – with safety pins or sewing pins, by tacking (basting) or with temporary spray glue. The sandwich is now ready for quilting. Remove pins or tacking when all of the quilting is finished.

BINDING

Binding finishes off a project nicely and provides a neat, durable edge. Double-fold binding is used for the projects in this book. Strips of fabric are cut 2¼in (6cm) or 2½in (6.5cm) wide, as per the project instructions.

1. Join the binding strips together end to end and press seams open. Fold the binding in half wrong sides together all along the length and press.

2. Pin the binding to the quilt by aligning the raw edges of the binding and quilt, a little way away from a corner. Using a ¼in (5mm) seam sew the binding in place, starting about 6in (15cm) away from the end of the binding. Stop ¼in (5mm) from the corner (Fig 4A). Take the quilt off the machine, rotate it and fold the binding upwards, creating a mitred corner (Fig 4B). Fold the binding back down, pinning it in place (Fig 4C). Begin sewing the seam again from the top to ¼in (5mm) from the next corner and then repeat the folding process. Do this on all corners. Before completing your stitching, neaten the short raw end of the starting piece and insert the ending piece into it.

3. Fold the binding over to the back of the quilt and neatly slipstitch in place by hand, creating neat mitres at each corner. Press to finish.

Fig 4

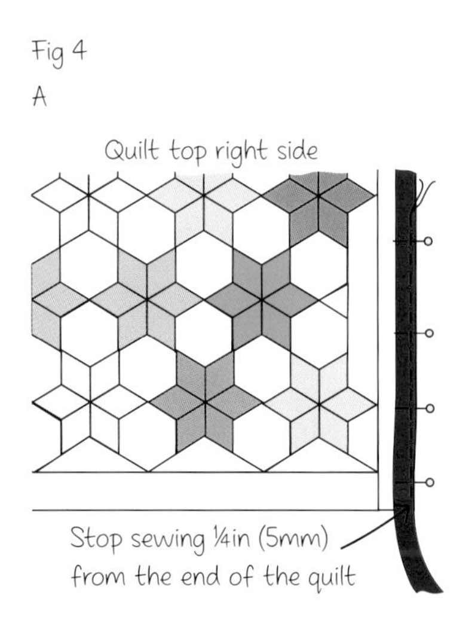

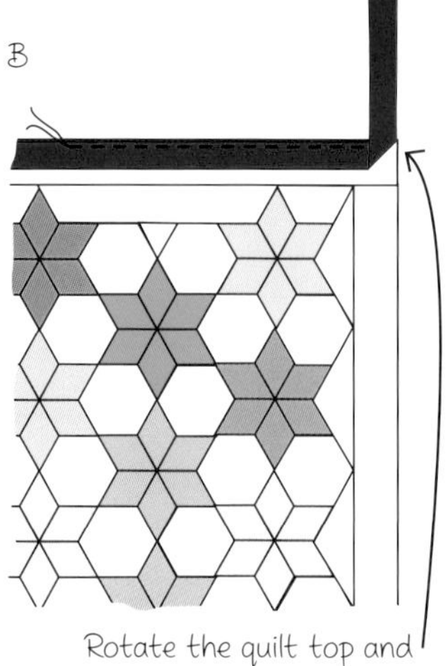

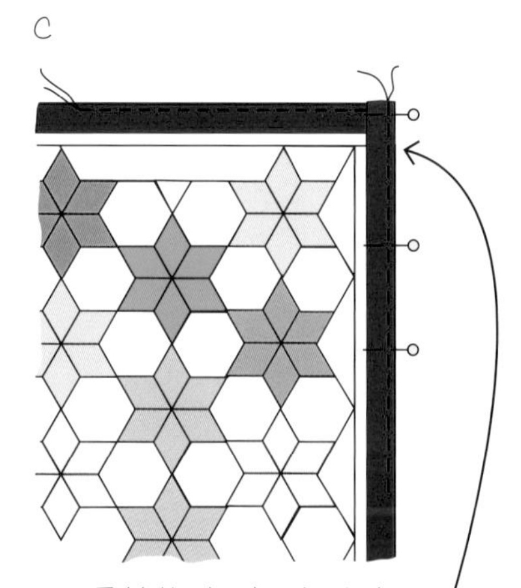

Backstitch

Backstitch can be used as an outline or to 'draw' features and details.

To work backstitch, bring the needle up through the fabric at 1 and down at 2, as shown on the diagram. Bring it back up at 3 and down at 4. Repeat the process to make further stitches.

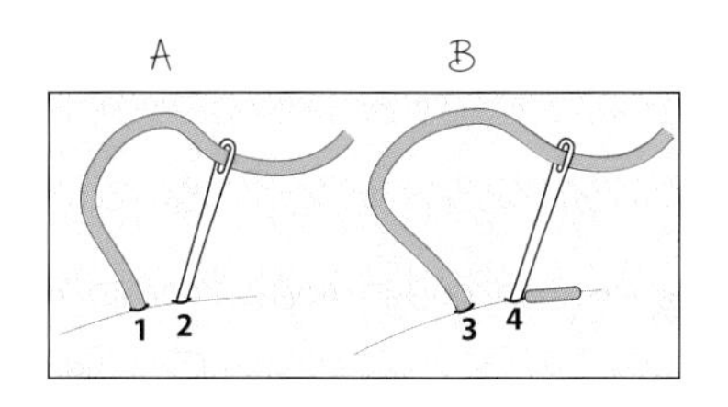

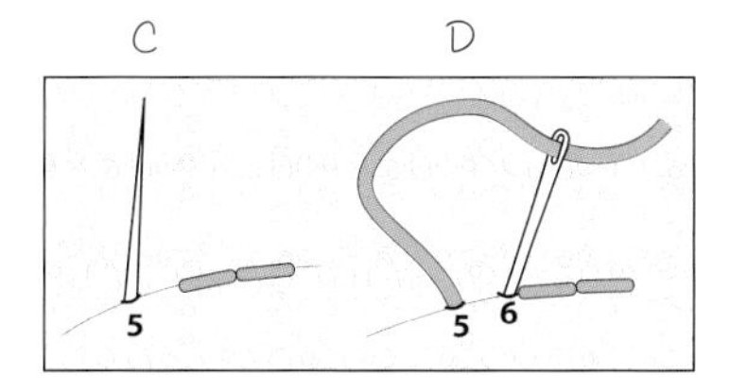

Blanket stitch

This stitch is used decoratively to edge appliqué motifs and can be spaced according to your preference. When very tightly spaced it is called buttonhole stitch.

To work blanket stitch, bring the needle and thread out on the edge of the appliqué motif and insert the needle as shown (Fig A). Pull the thread through so a loop forms (B). Put the needle through the loop and pull the thread so that it lies snugly against the appliqué edge (C). Continue in the same way, following the outline of the motif you are edging (D).

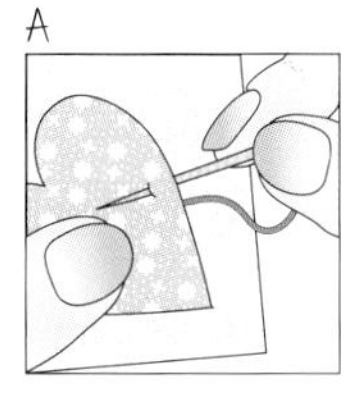

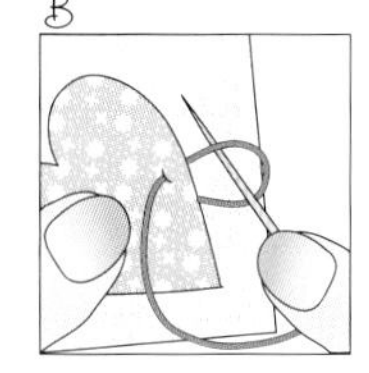

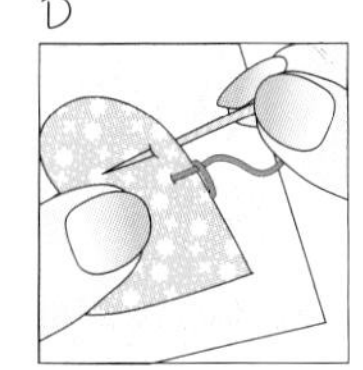

French knot

This is a useful little stitch that can be used to add detail or texture. In this book they are usually worked with two strands of thread wound once or twice around the needle.

To work a French knot, bring the needle up to the right side of the fabric, hold the thread down with your finger and wind the thread round the needle once or twice (A). Still holding the thread taut put the needle through to the back of the work a short distance away from the entry point (B). Pull the thread to tighten the knot (C). For bigger knots, use more strands of thread.

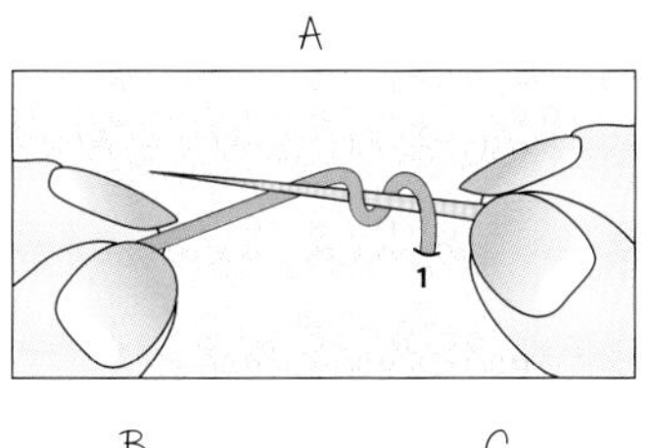

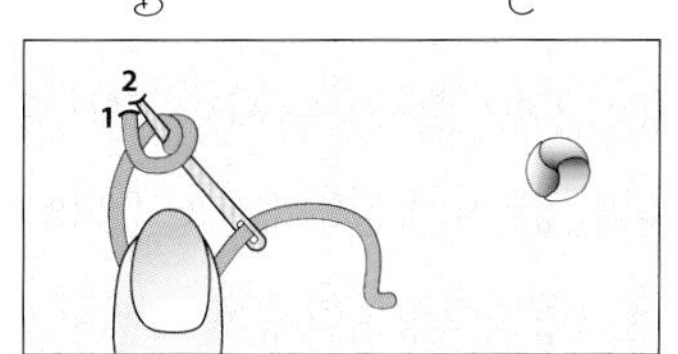

Running stitch

A long running stitch can be used to gather fabrics, while a shorter running stitch is used for quilting. You don't have to work small stitches when quilting – find the length that suits you.

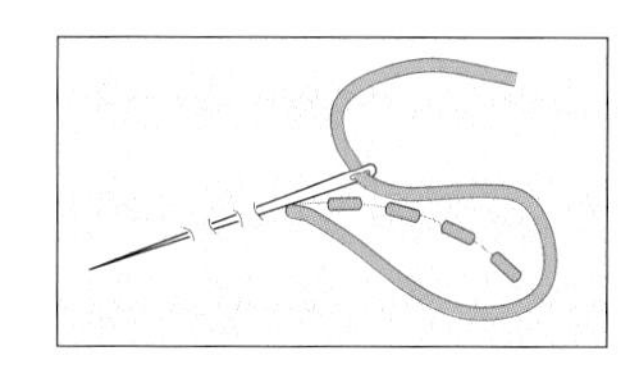

Satin stitch

Satin stitch is normally used as a filling stitch to give blocks of thread colour. It is used for facial details in the delightful Little Bear toy. Work the stitches side by side closely together, as shown in diagrams A to D.

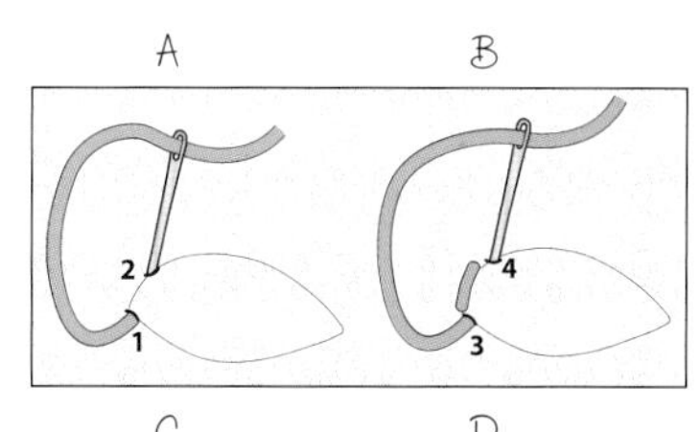

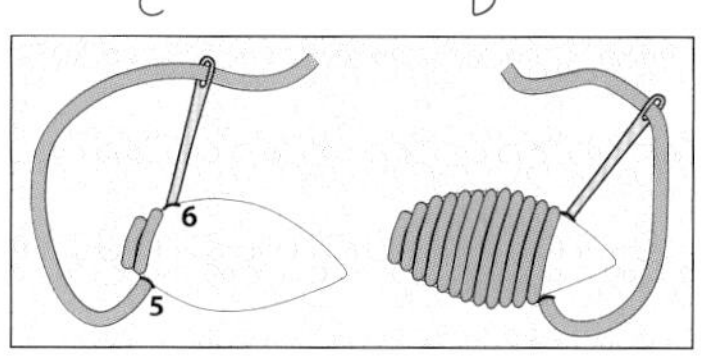

Attaching beads

Attach beads using a beading needle or very fine 'sharp' needle. Use thread that matches the bead colour and secure well.

ABOUT THE AUTHOR

Helen Philipps studied printed textiles and embroidery at Manchester Metropolitan University and then taught drawing and design before becoming a freelance designer. After working in the greetings industry, Helen's love of needlecraft led her to create original designs for stitching magazines and books. Her work features regularly in many stitch and craft magazines and she also writes a popular craft blog: helenphilipps.blogspot.co.uk. This is Helen's ninth book for David & Charles, following on from *Pretty Patchwork Gifts* published in 2013.

SUPPLIERS

Fat Quarter Shop
www.fatquartershop.com

Fred Aldous
www.fredaldous.co.uk

Hobbycraft
www.hobbycraft.co.uk
For a wide range of supplies

Longarm Quilting
www.longarmquilting.co.uk

Plush Addict
www.plushaddict.co.uk

Sew and Quilt
www.sewandquilt.co.uk
For pre-cut templates

Sew and So
www.sewandso.co.uk
For buttons and embellishments

StitchCraftCreate
www.stitchcraftcreate.co.uk
For fabrics and embellishments

ACKNOWLEDGMENTS

Thank you to everyone at David & Charles for all their hard work and creative skills in producing this book. Thank you to Ame Verso for commissioning the book and for all her ideas and input. Thank you to my wonderful editor Lin Clements whose patience, editing skills and attention to detail always make working with her so pleasant and easy. Thank you to Honor Head for all her help and for keeping things so well organized. Thank you to Anna Fazakerley and Lorraine Inglis for the beautiful book design and styling and thank you of course to Pru Rogers for the art direction and Jason Jenkins for the stunning photography.

Finally, thanks to my lovely husband David and all my family, for all their love, support and encouragement.

INDEX

A DAVID & CHARLES BOOK

David & Charles is an imprint of F&W Media International, Ltd
Brunel House, Forde Close, Newton Abbot, TQ12 4PU, UK

F&W Media International, Ltd is a subsidiary of F+W Media, Inc
10151 Carver Road, Suite #200, Blue Ash, OH 45242, USA

First published in the UK and USA in 2015

A catalogue record for this book is available from the British Library.

ISBN-13: 978-1-4463-0598-0 paperback
ISBN-10: 1-4463-0598-8 paperback

ISBN-13: 978-1-4463-7258-6 EPUB
ISBN-10: 1-4463-7258-8 EPUB

ISBN-13: 978-1-4463-7259-3 PDF
ISBN-10: 1-4463-7259-6 PDF

Printed in China by RR Donnelley for:
F&W Media International, Ltd
Brunel House, Forde Close, Newton Abbot, TQ12 4PU, UK

10 9 8 7 6 5 4 3 2 1

Acquisitions Editor: Ame Verso
Managing Editor: Honor Head
Project Editor: Lin Clements
Art Editor: Anna Fazakerley
Designer: Lorraine Inglis
Photographer: Jason Jenkins
Art Direction: Prudence Rogers
Location hire: 'Bessie' the vintage caravan at Woods Farm Holiday Park, Bude, Cornwall www.wooda.co.uk
Prop hire: www.devonvintagehire.co.uk
Production Manager: Beverley Richardson

Layout of the digital edition of this book may vary depending on reader hardware and display settings.